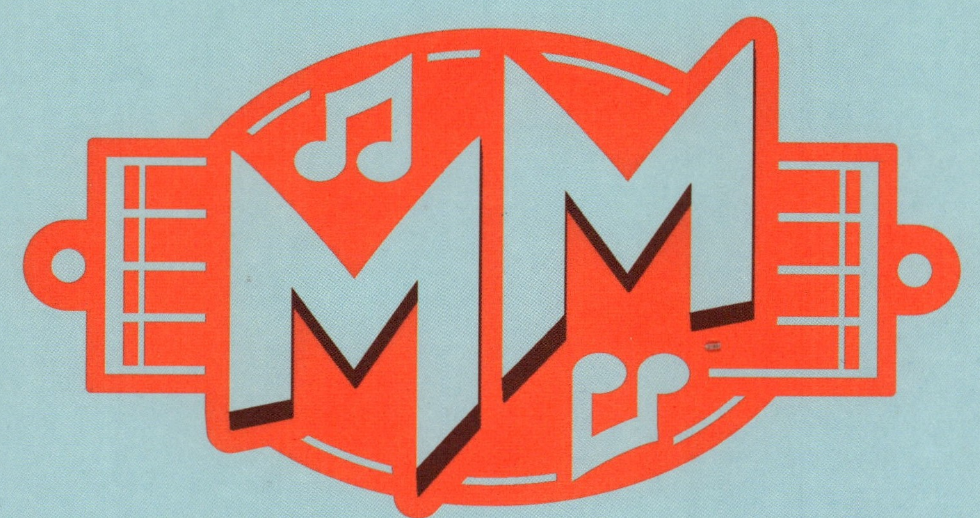

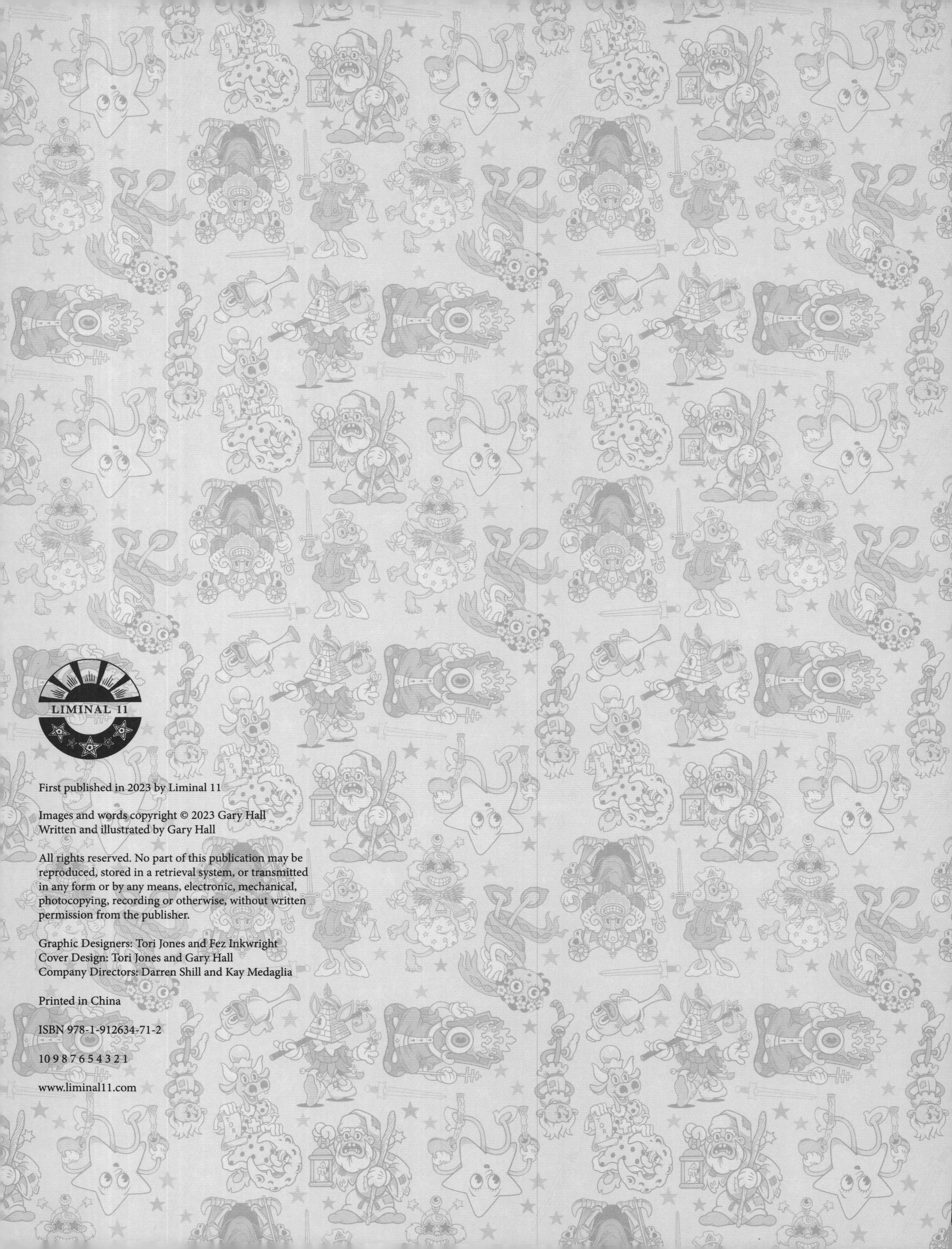

First published in 2023 by Liminal 11

Graphic Designers: Tori Jones and Fez Inkwright
Cover Design: Tori Jones and Gary Hall
Company Directors: Darren Shill and Kay Medaglia

Printed in China

ISBN 978-1-912634-71-2

10 9 8 7 6 5 4 3 2 1

www.liminal11.com

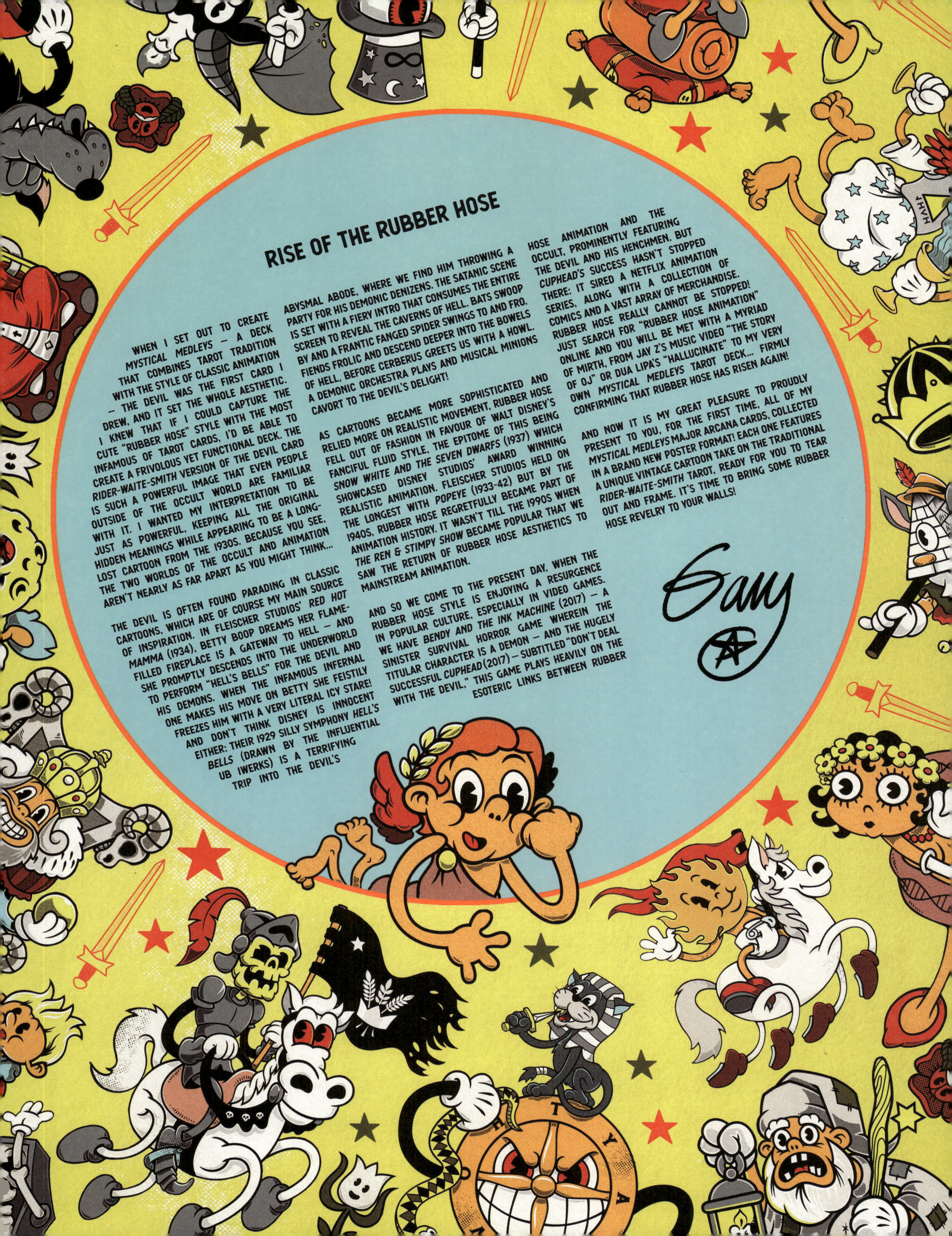

RISE OF THE RUBBER HOSE

WHEN I SET OUT TO CREATE MYSTICAL MEDLEYS — A DECK THAT COMBINES TAROT TRADITION WITH THE STYLE OF CLASSIC ANIMATION — THE DEVIL WAS THE FIRST CARD I DREW, AND IT SET THE WHOLE AESTHETIC. I KNEW THAT IF I COULD CAPTURE THE CUTE "RUBBER HOSE" STYLE WITH THE MOST INFAMOUS OF TAROT CARDS, I'D BE ABLE TO CREATE A FRIVOLOUS YET FUNCTIONAL DECK. THE RIDER-WAITE-SMITH VERSION OF THE DEVIL CARD IS SUCH A POWERFUL IMAGE THAT EVEN PEOPLE OUTSIDE OF THE OCCULT WORLD ARE FAMILIAR WITH IT. I WANTED MY INTERPRETATION TO BE JUST AS POWERFUL, KEEPING ALL THE ORIGINAL HIDDEN MEANINGS WHILE APPEARING TO BE A LONG-LOST CARTOON FROM THE 1930S. BECAUSE YOU SEE, THE TWO WORLDS OF THE OCCULT AND ANIMATION AREN'T NEARLY AS FAR APART AS YOU MIGHT THINK...

THE DEVIL IS OFTEN FOUND PARADING IN CLASSIC CARTOONS, WHICH ARE OF COURSE MY MAIN SOURCE OF INSPIRATION. IN FLEISCHER STUDIOS' *RED HOT MAMMA* (1934), BETTY BOOP DREAMS HER FLAME-FILLED FIREPLACE IS A GATEWAY TO HELL — AND SHE PROMPTLY DESCENDS INTO THE UNDERWORLD TO PERFORM "HELL'S BELLS" FOR THE DEVIL AND HIS DEMONS. WHEN THE INFAMOUS INFERNAL ONE MAKES HIS MOVE ON BETTY SHE FEISTILY FREEZES HIM WITH A VERY LITERAL ICY STARE! AND DON'T THINK DISNEY IS INNOCENT EITHER: THEIR 1929 SILLY SYMPHONY *HELL'S BELLS* (DRAWN BY THE INFLUENTIAL UB IWERKS) IS A TERRIFYING TRIP INTO THE DEVIL'S

ABYSMAL ABODE, WHERE WE FIND HIM THROWING A PARTY FOR HIS DEMONIC DENIZENS. THE SATANIC SCENE IS SET WITH A FIERY INTRO THAT CONSUMES THE ENTIRE SCREEN TO REVEAL THE CAVERNS OF HELL. BATS SWOOP BY AND A FRANTIC FANGED SPIDER SWINGS TO AND FRO. FIENDS FROLIC AND DESCEND DEEPER INTO THE BOWELS OF HELL, BEFORE CERBERUS GREETS US WITH A HOWL. A DEMONIC ORCHESTRA PLAYS AND MUSICAL MINIONS CAVORT TO THE DEVIL'S DELIGHT!

AS CARTOONS BECAME MORE SOPHISTICATED AND RELIED MORE ON REALISTIC MOVEMENT, RUBBER HOSE FELL OUT OF FASHION IN FAVOUR OF WALT DISNEY'S FANCIFUL FLUID STYLE, THE EPITOME OF THIS BEING *SNOW WHITE AND THE SEVEN DWARFS* (1937) WHICH SHOWCASED DISNEY STUDIOS' AWARD WINNING REALISTIC ANIMATION. FLEISCHER STUDIOS HELD ON THE LONGEST WITH *POPEYE* (1933-42) BUT BY THE 1940S, RUBBER HOSE REGRETFULLY BECAME PART OF ANIMATION HISTORY. IT WASN'T TILL THE 1990S WHEN THE *REN & STIMPY* SHOW BECAME POPULAR THAT WE SAW THE RETURN OF RUBBER HOSE AESTHETICS TO MAINSTREAM ANIMATION.

AND SO WE COME TO THE PRESENT DAY, WHEN THE RUBBER HOSE STYLE IS ENJOYING A RESURGENCE IN POPULAR CULTURE, ESPECIALLY IN VIDEO GAMES. WE HAVE *BENDY AND THE INK MACHINE* (2017) — A SINISTER SURVIVAL HORROR GAME WHEREIN THE TITULAR CHARACTER IS A DEMON — AND THE HUGELY SUCCESSFUL *CUPHEAD* (2017) — SUBTITLED "DON'T DEAL WITH THE DEVIL," THIS GAME PLAYS HEAVILY ON THE ESOTERIC LINKS BETWEEN RUBBER HOSE ANIMATION AND THE OCCULT, PROMINENTLY FEATURING THE DEVIL AND HIS HENCHMEN. BUT *CUPHEAD*'S SUCCESS HASN'T STOPPED THERE: IT SIRED A NETFLIX ANIMATION SERIES, ALONG WITH A COLLECTION OF COMICS AND A VAST ARRAY OF MERCHANDISE. RUBBER HOSE REALLY CANNOT BE STOPPED! JUST SEARCH FOR "RUBBER HOSE ANIMATION" ONLINE AND YOU WILL BE MET WITH A MYRIAD OF MIRTH, FROM JAY Z'S MUSIC VIDEO "THE STORY OF OJ" OR DUA LIPA'S "HALLUCINATE" TO MY VERY OWN MYSTICAL MEDLEYS TAROT DECK... FIRMLY CONFIRMING THAT RUBBER HOSE HAS RISEN AGAIN!

AND NOW IT IS MY GREAT PLEASURE TO PROUDLY PRESENT TO YOU, FOR THE FIRST TIME, ALL OF MY MYSTICAL MEDLEYS MAJOR ARCANA CARDS, COLLECTED IN A BRAND NEW POSTER FORMAT! EACH ONE FEATURES A UNIQUE VINTAGE CARTOON TAKE ON THE TRADITIONAL *RIDER-WAITE-SMITH* TAROT, READY FOR YOU TO TEAR OUT AND FRAME. IT'S TIME TO BRING SOME RUBBER HOSE REVELRY TO YOUR WALLS!

Gary

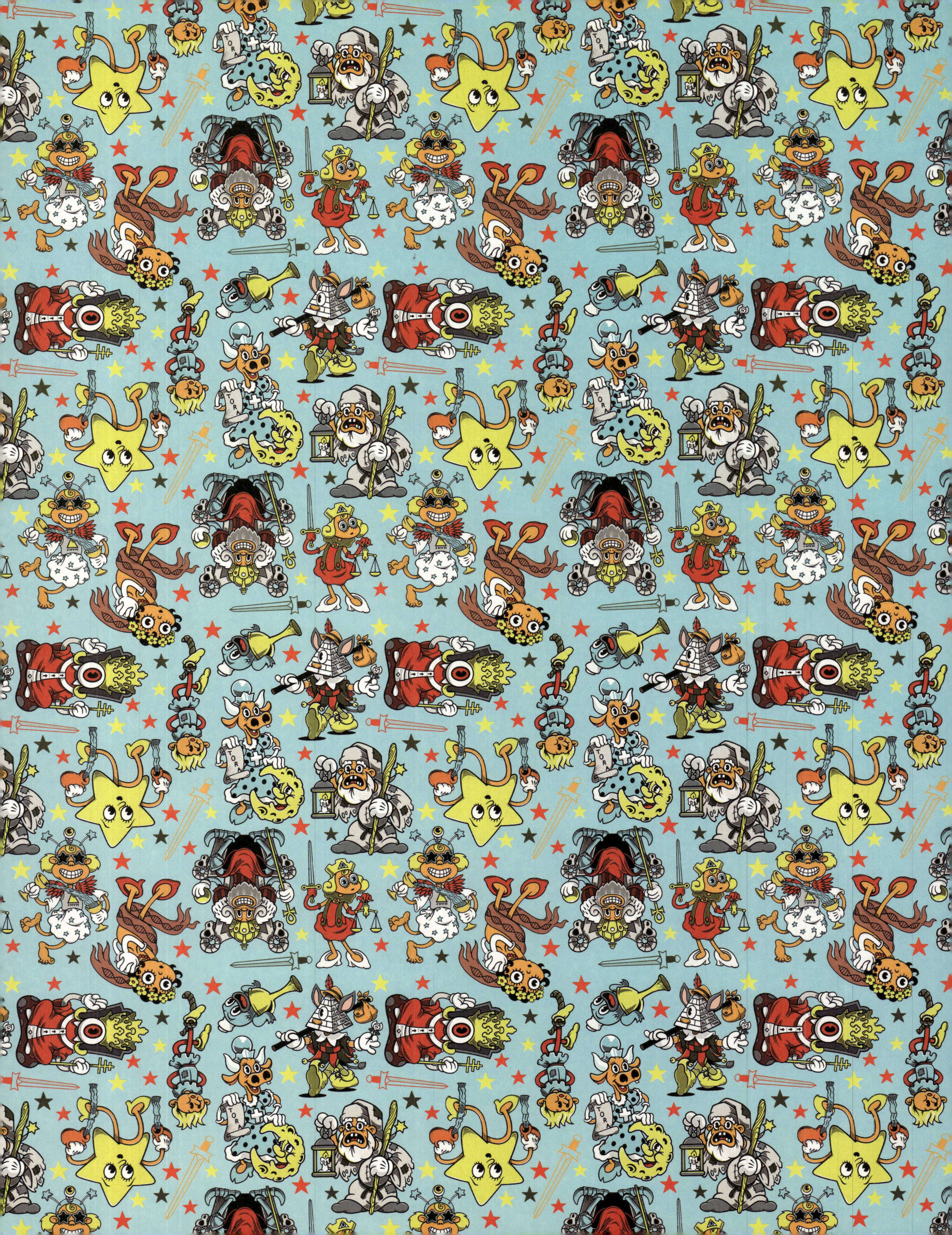

O

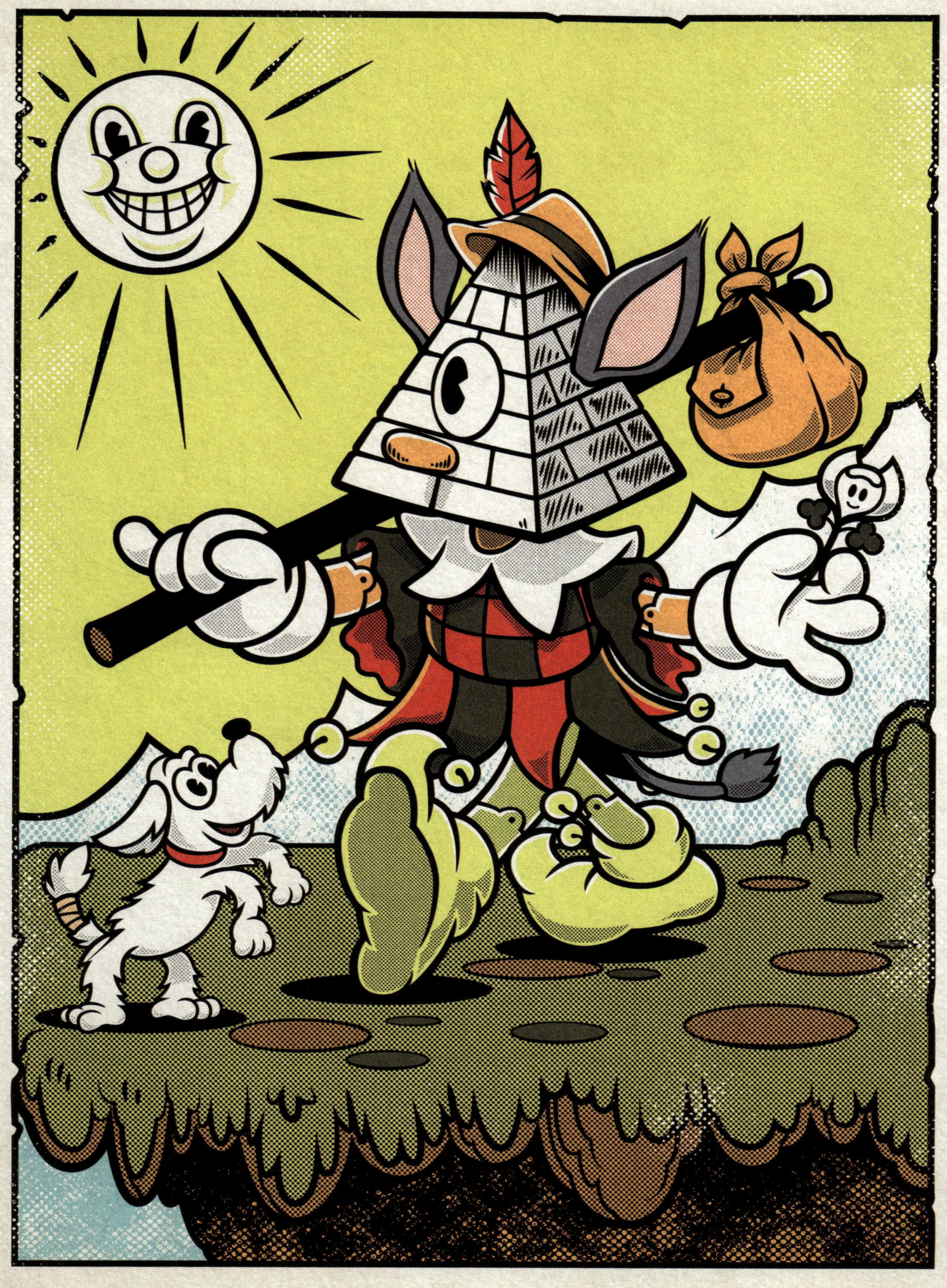

THE FOOL

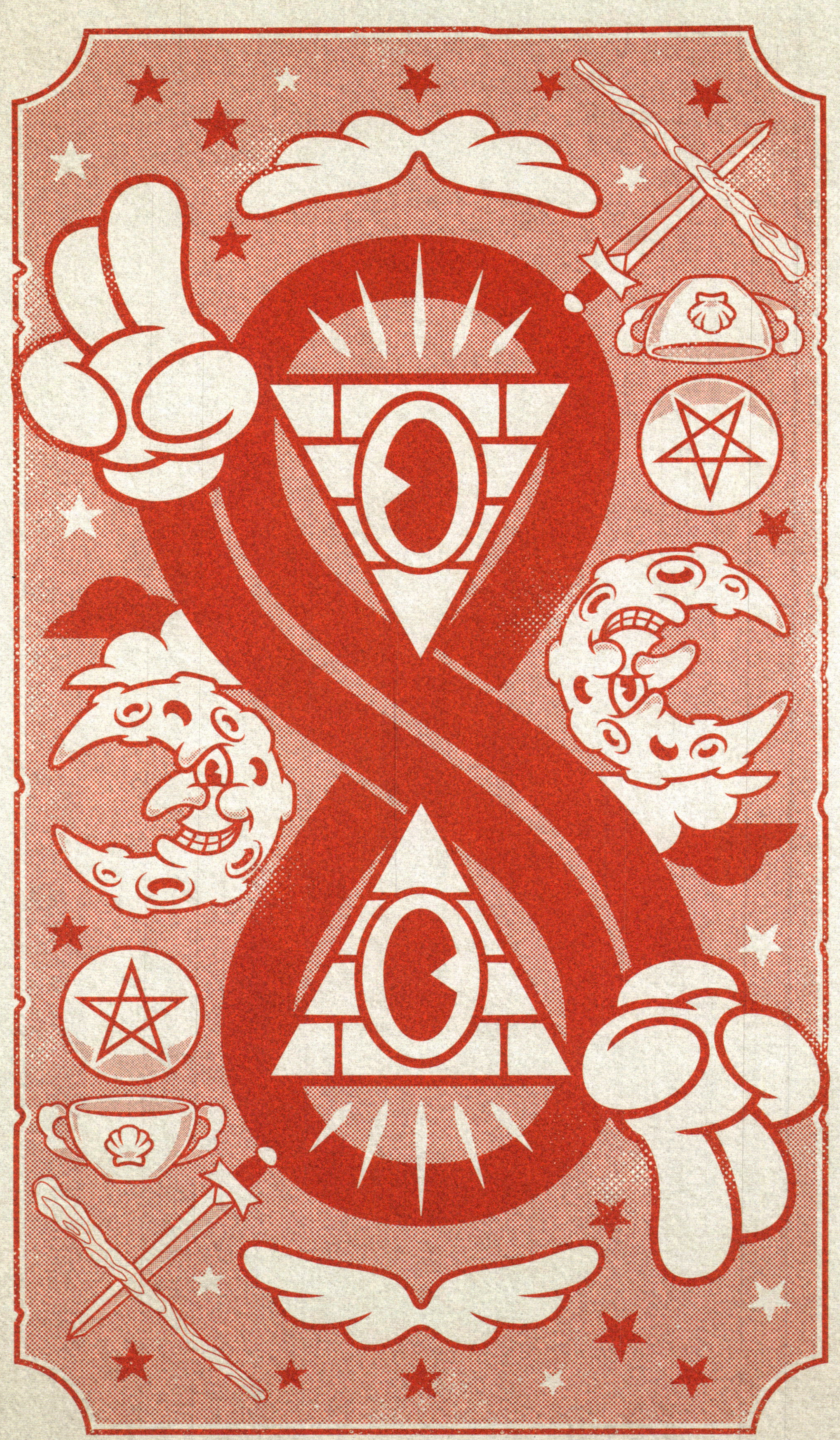

I

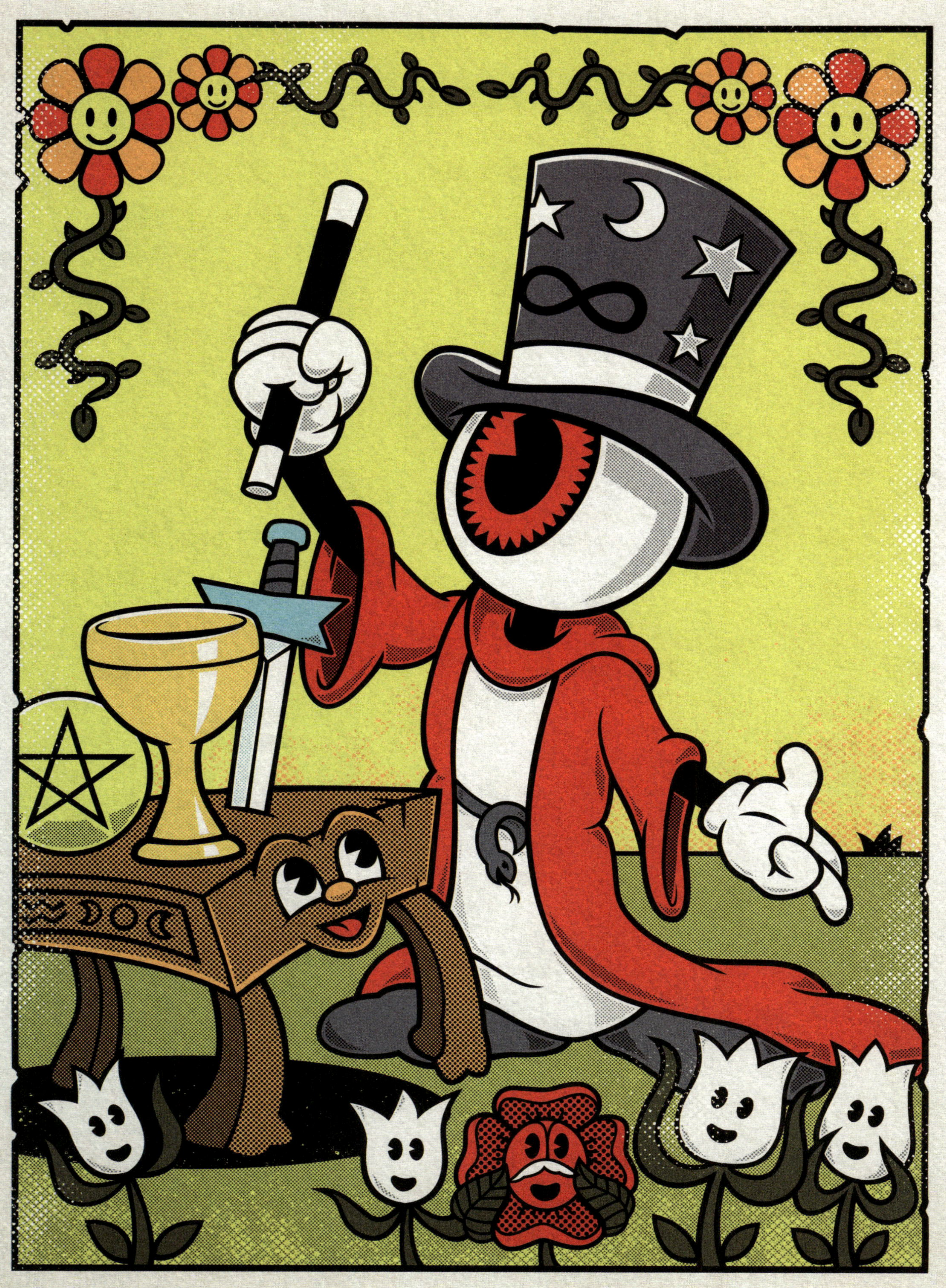

THE MAGICIAN

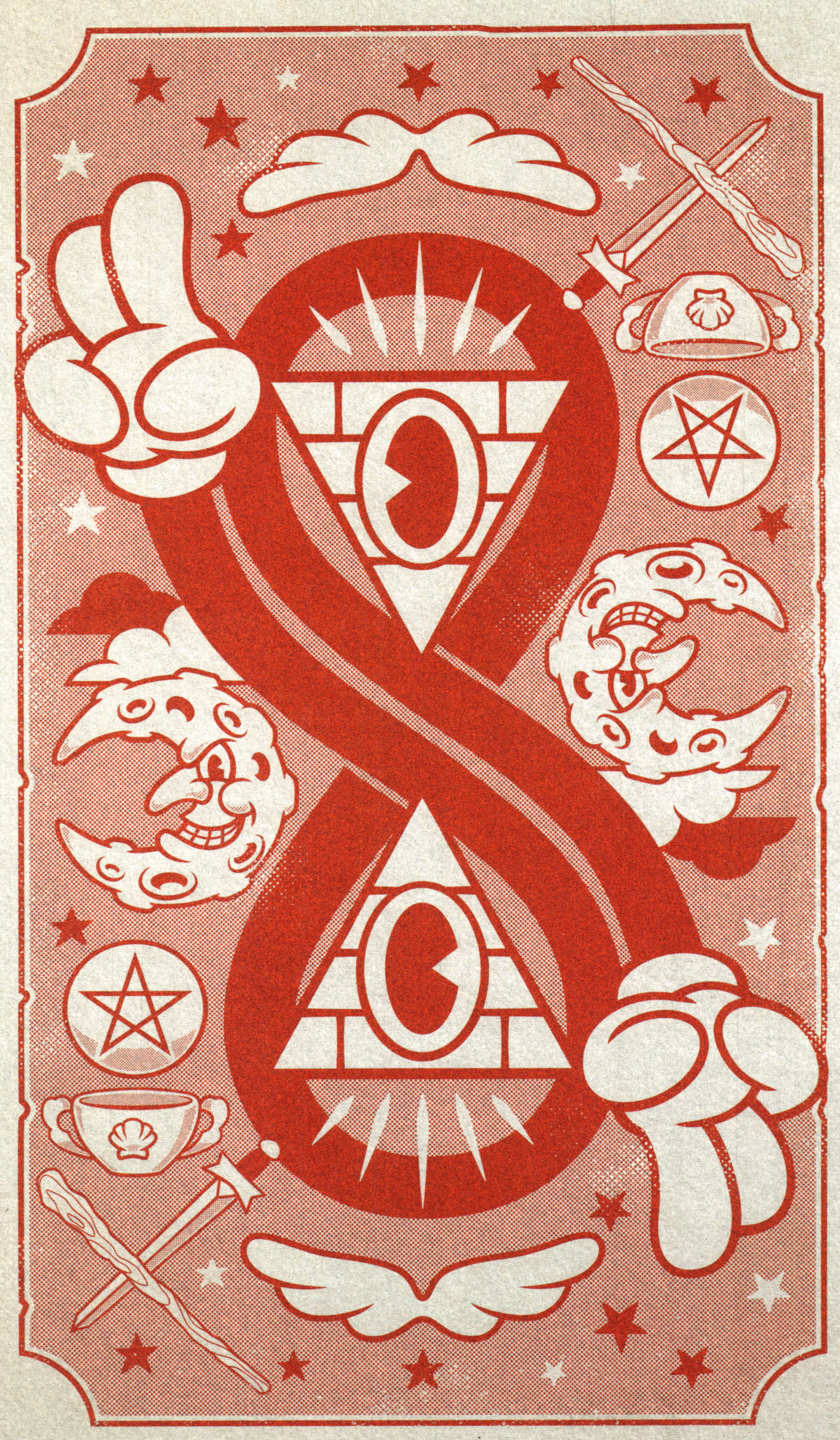

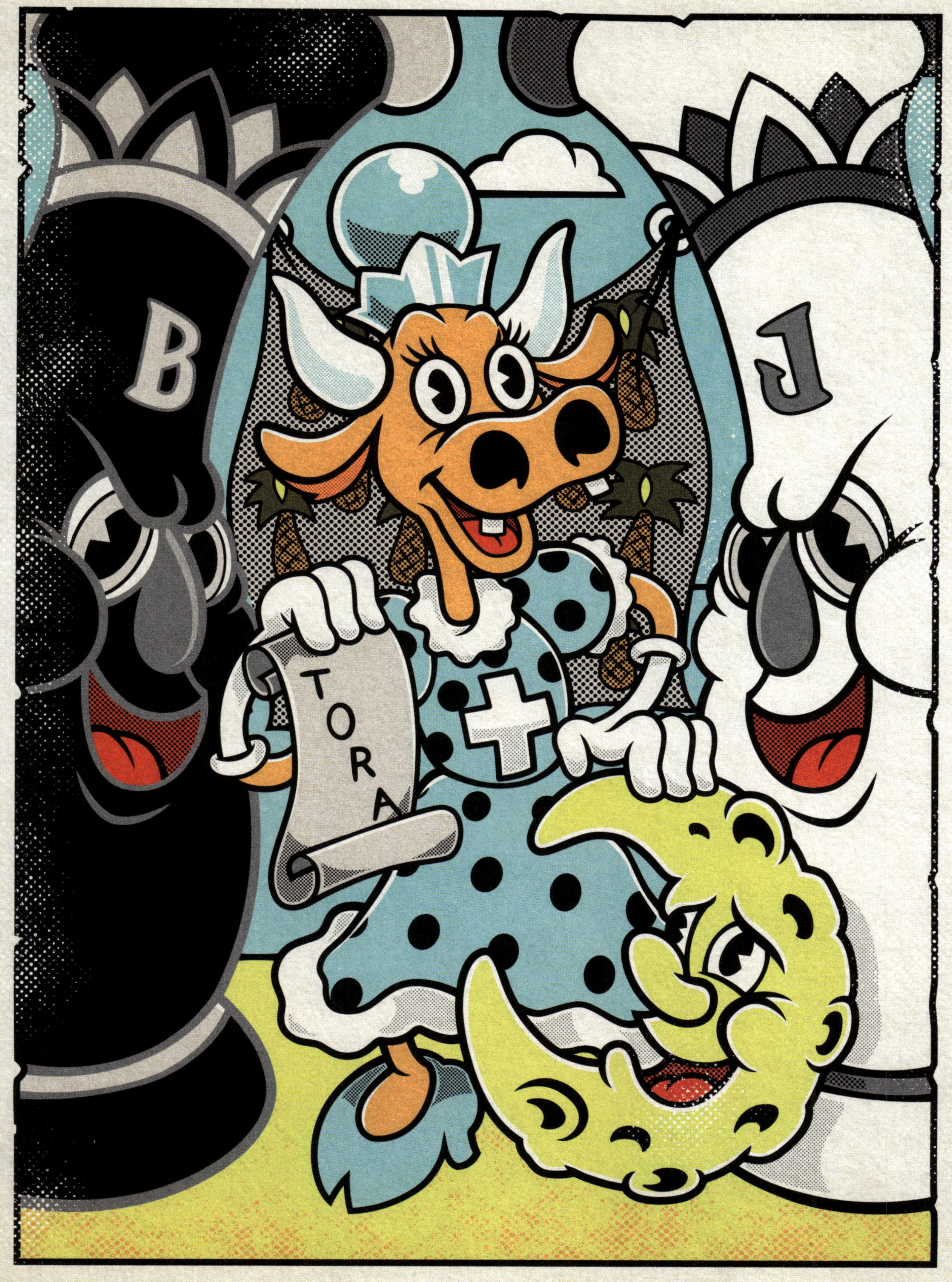

THE HIGH PRIESTESS

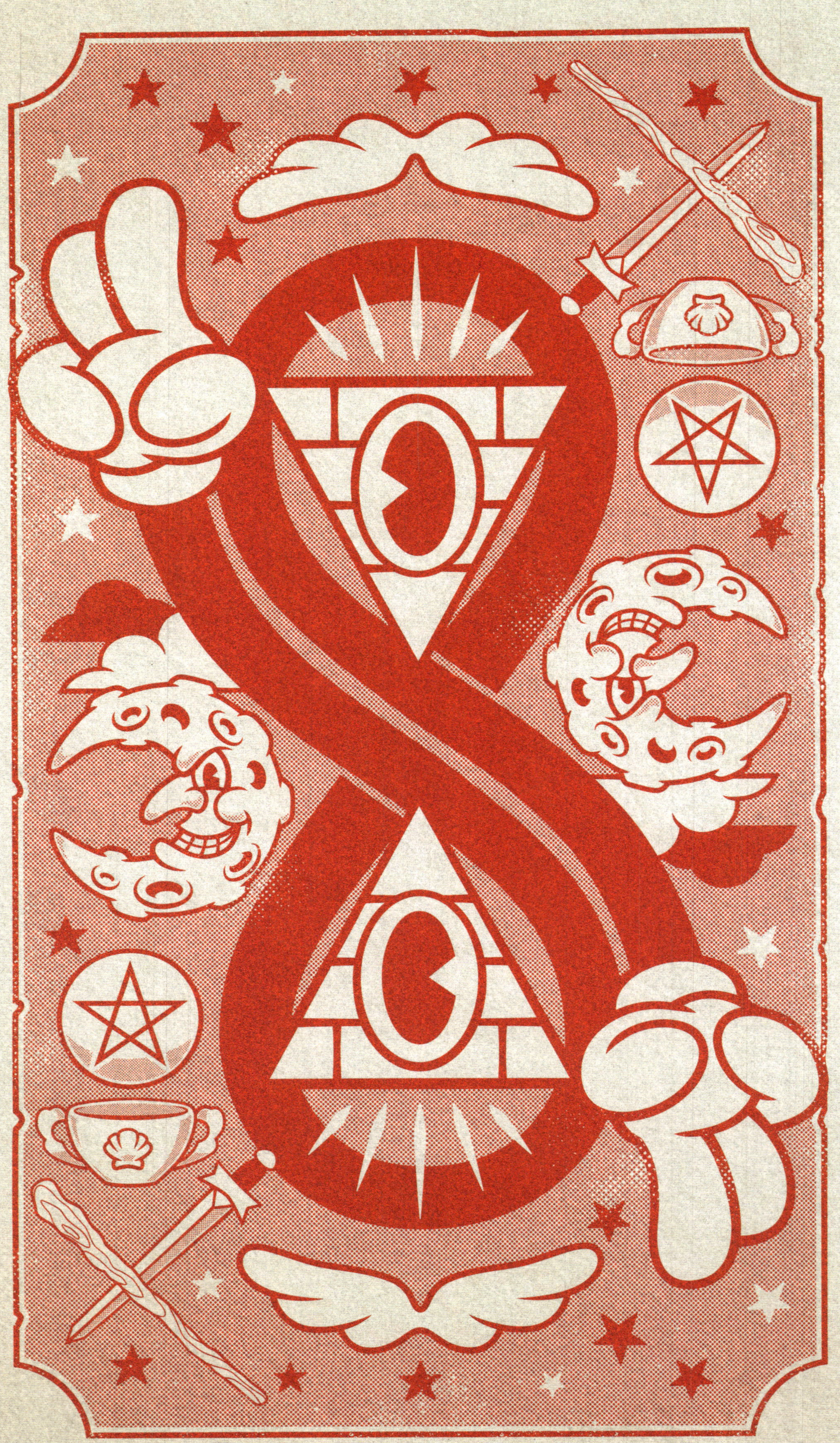

III

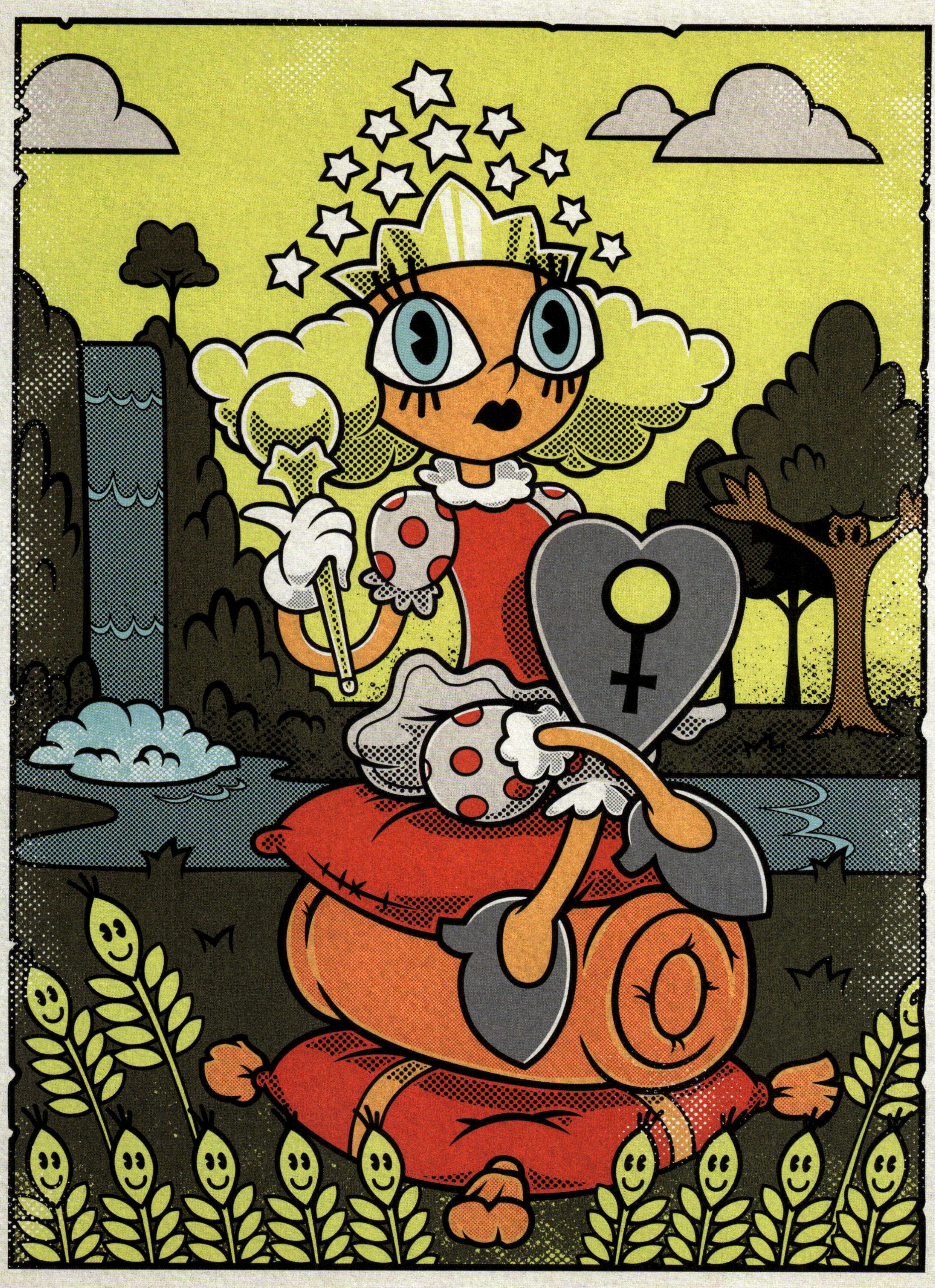

THE EMPRESS

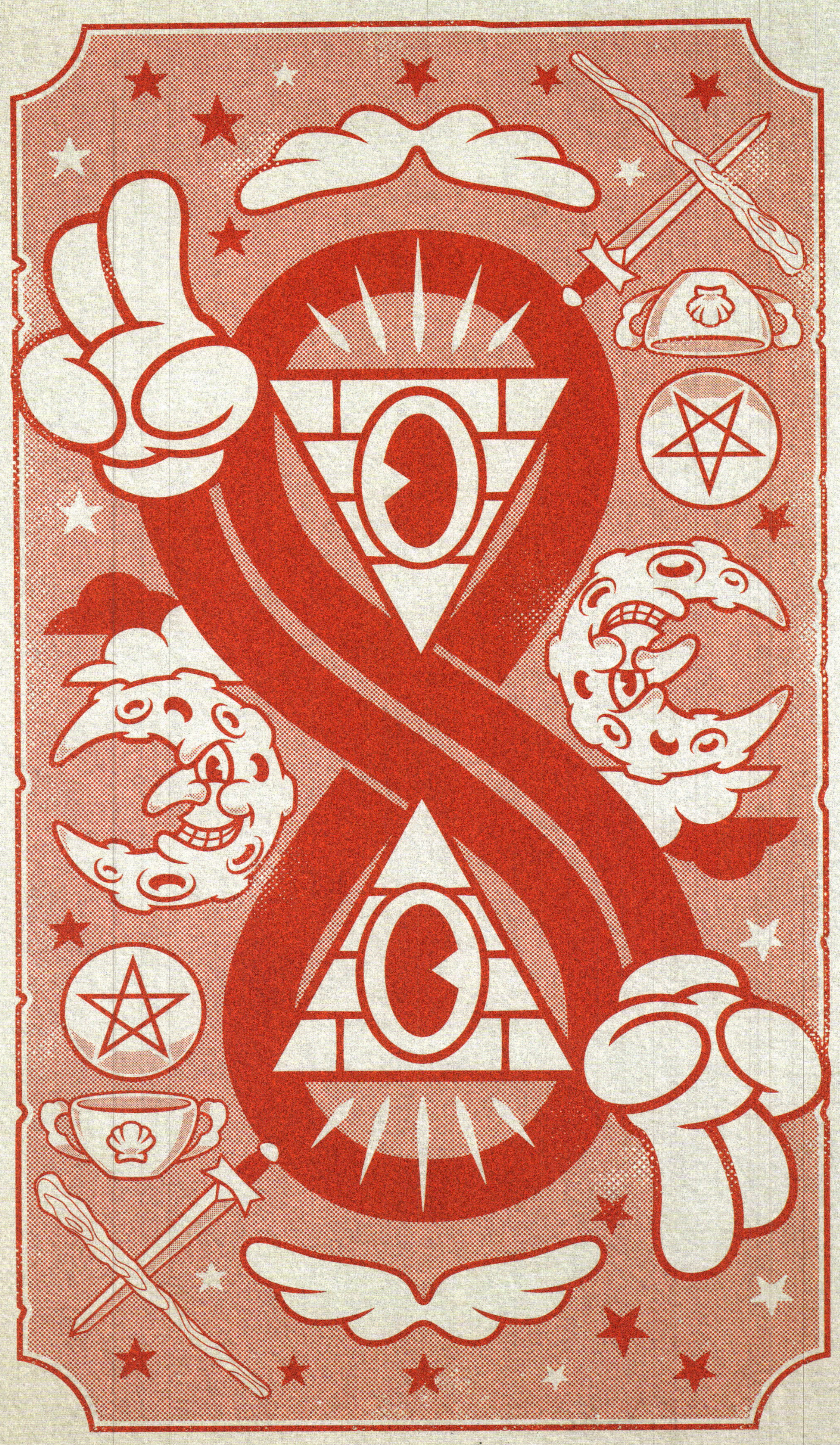

IV

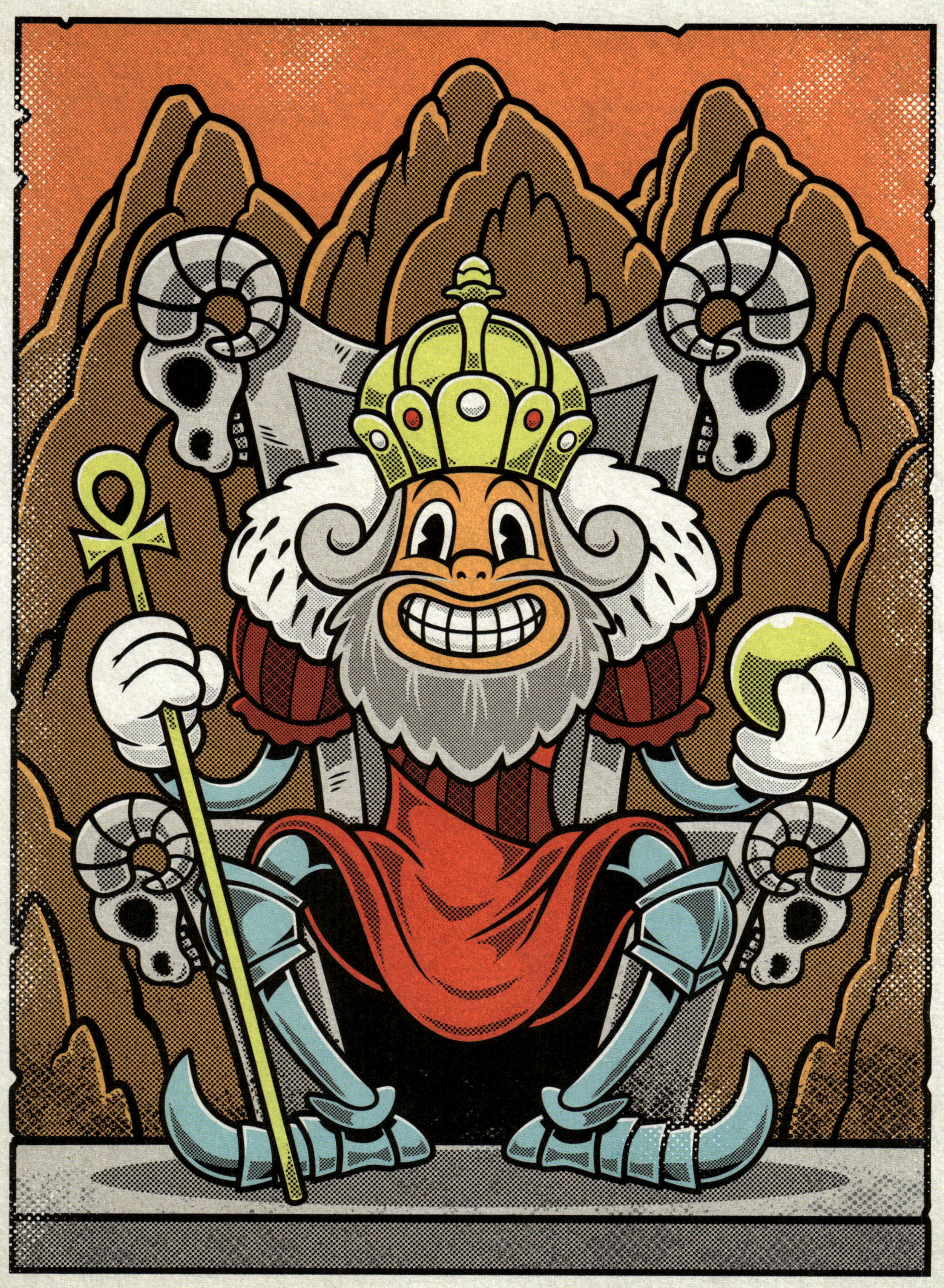

THE EMPEROR

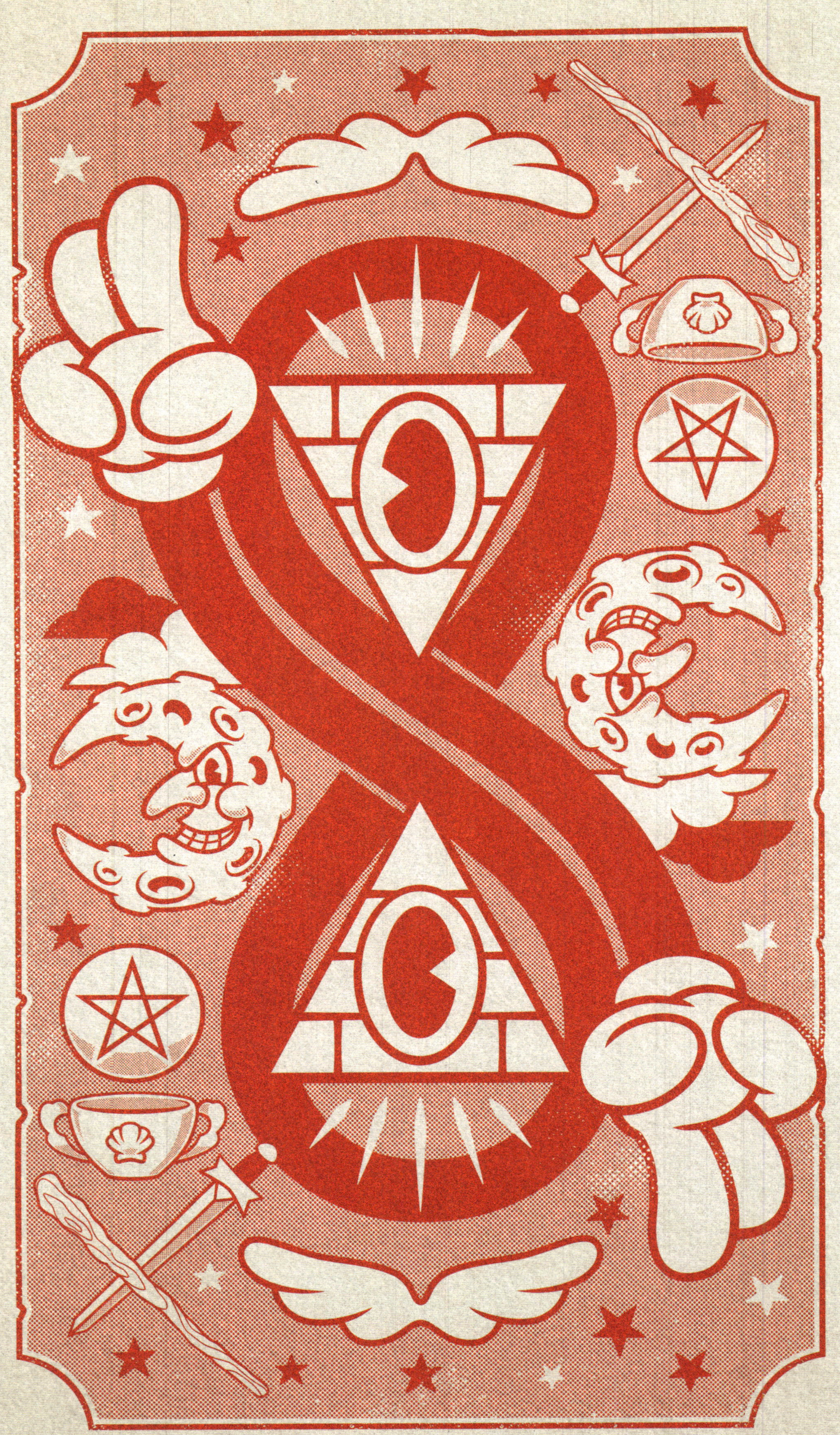

V

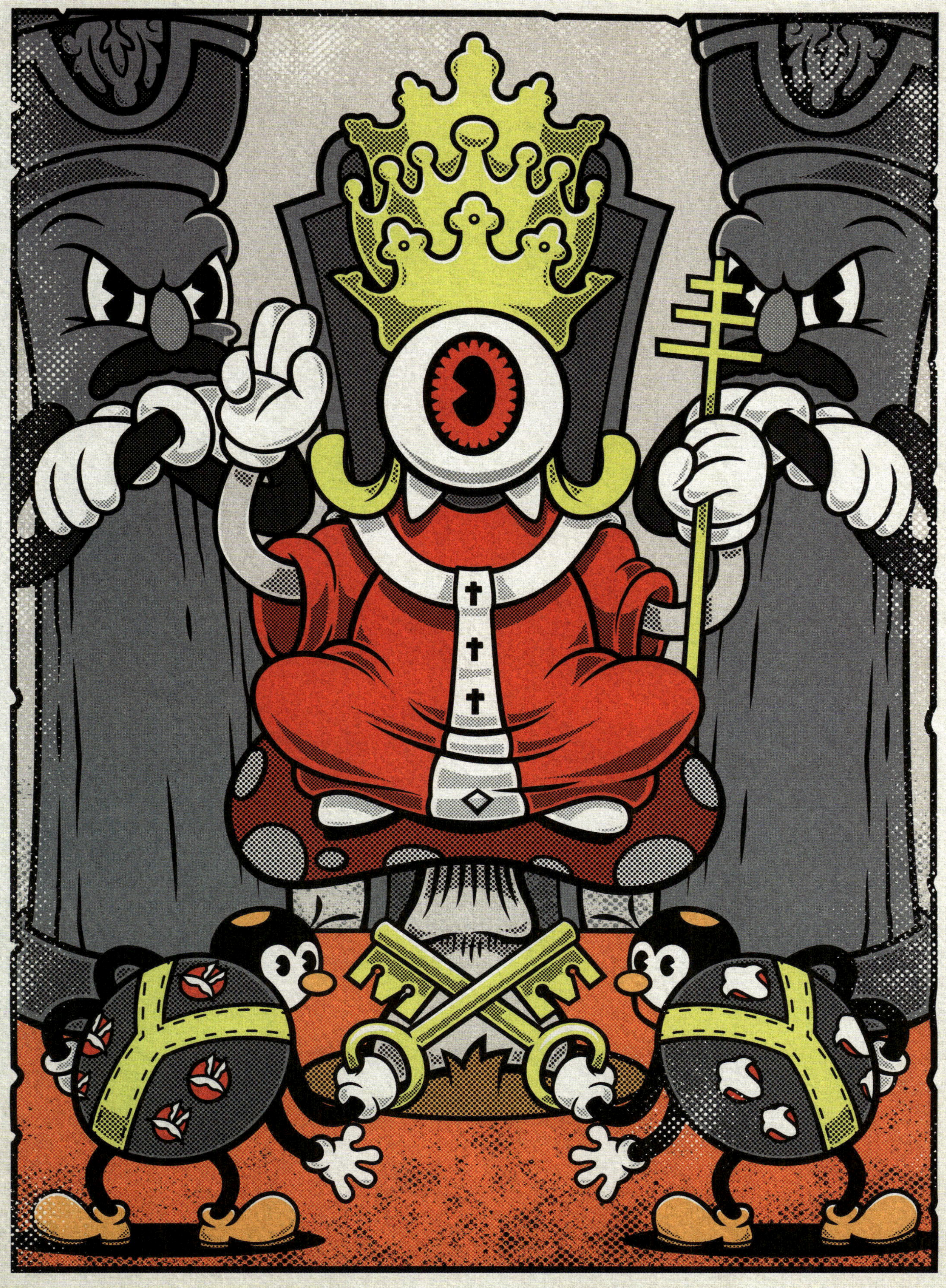

THE HIEROPHANT

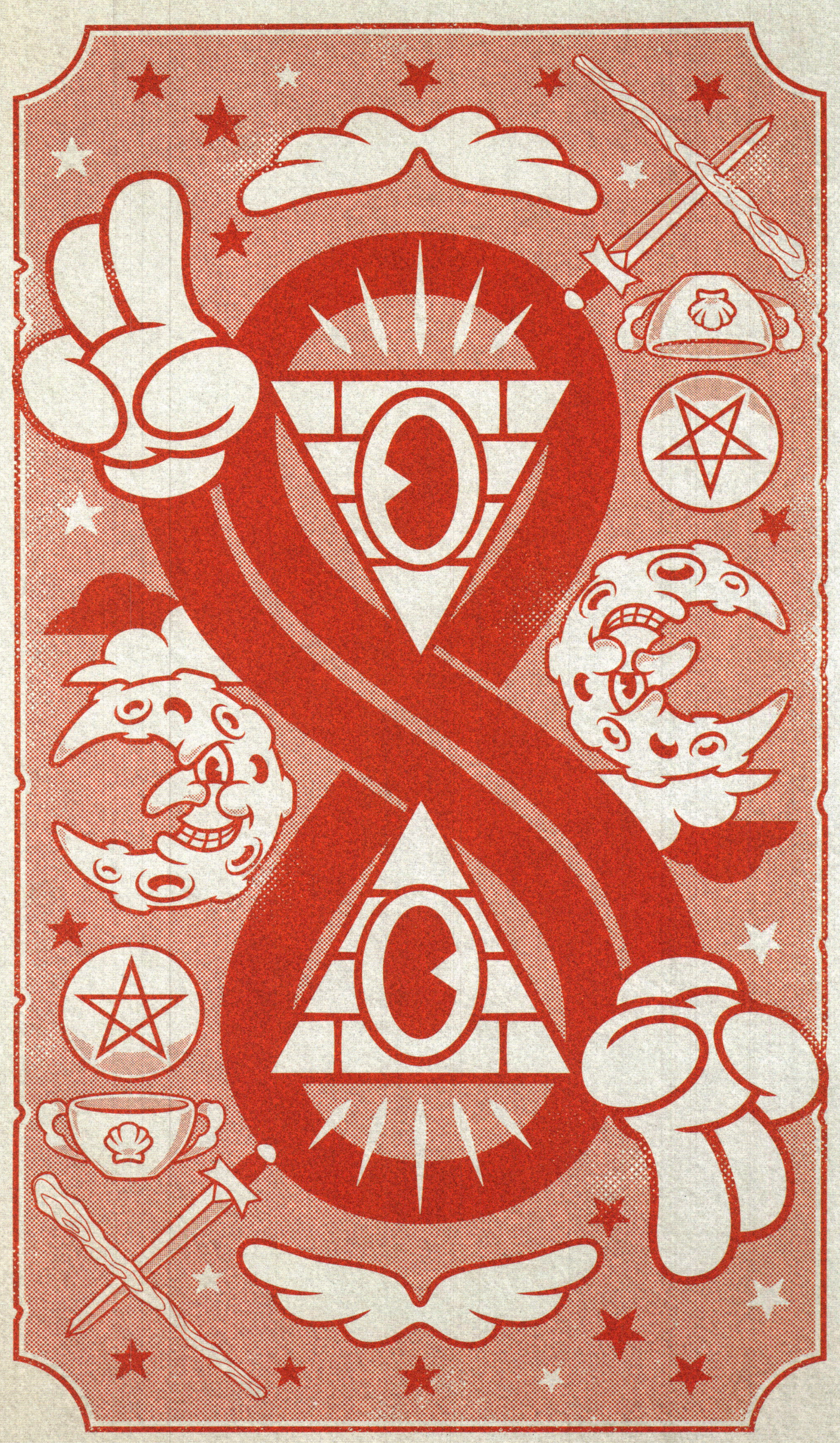

VI

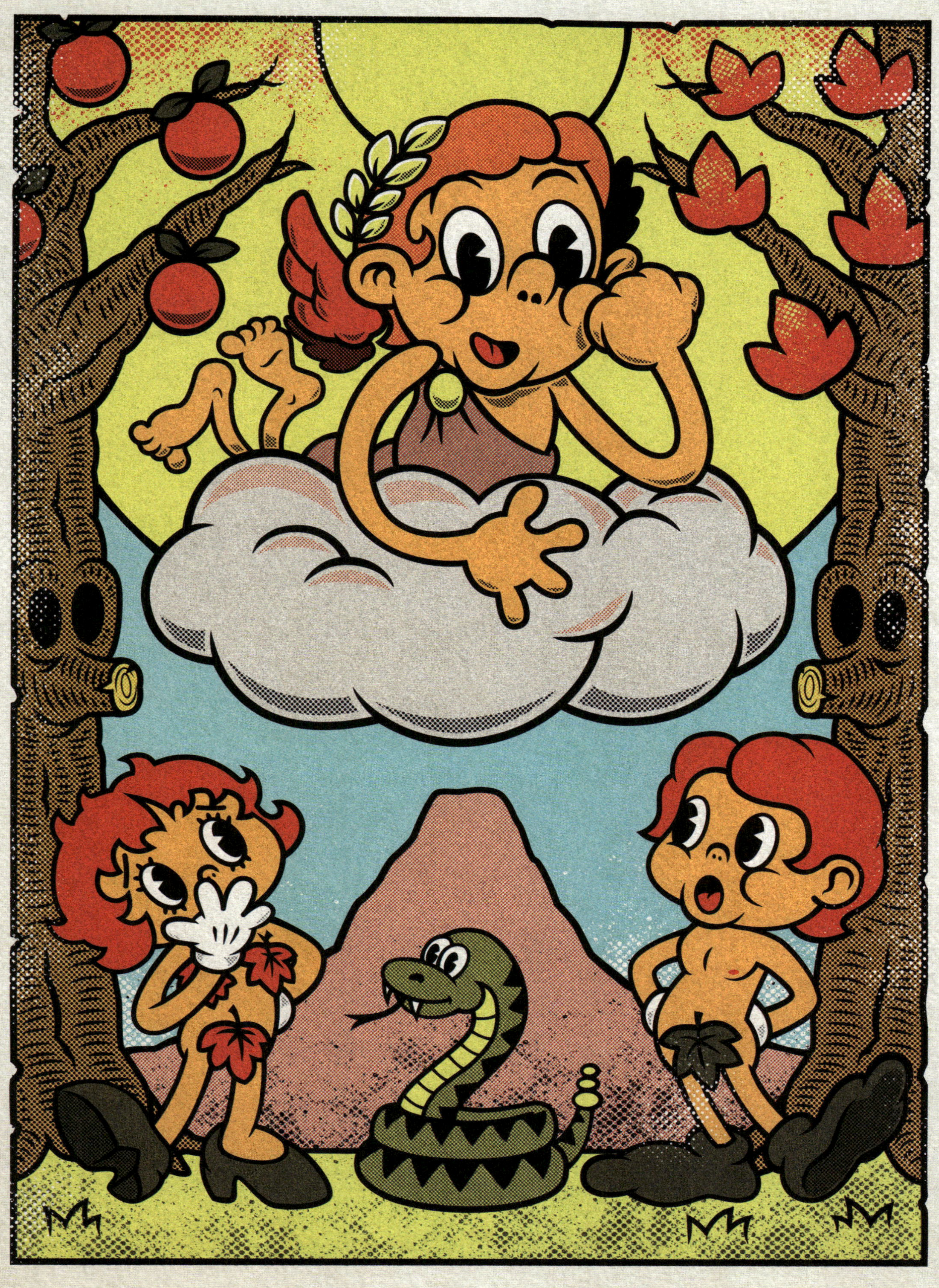

THE LOVERS

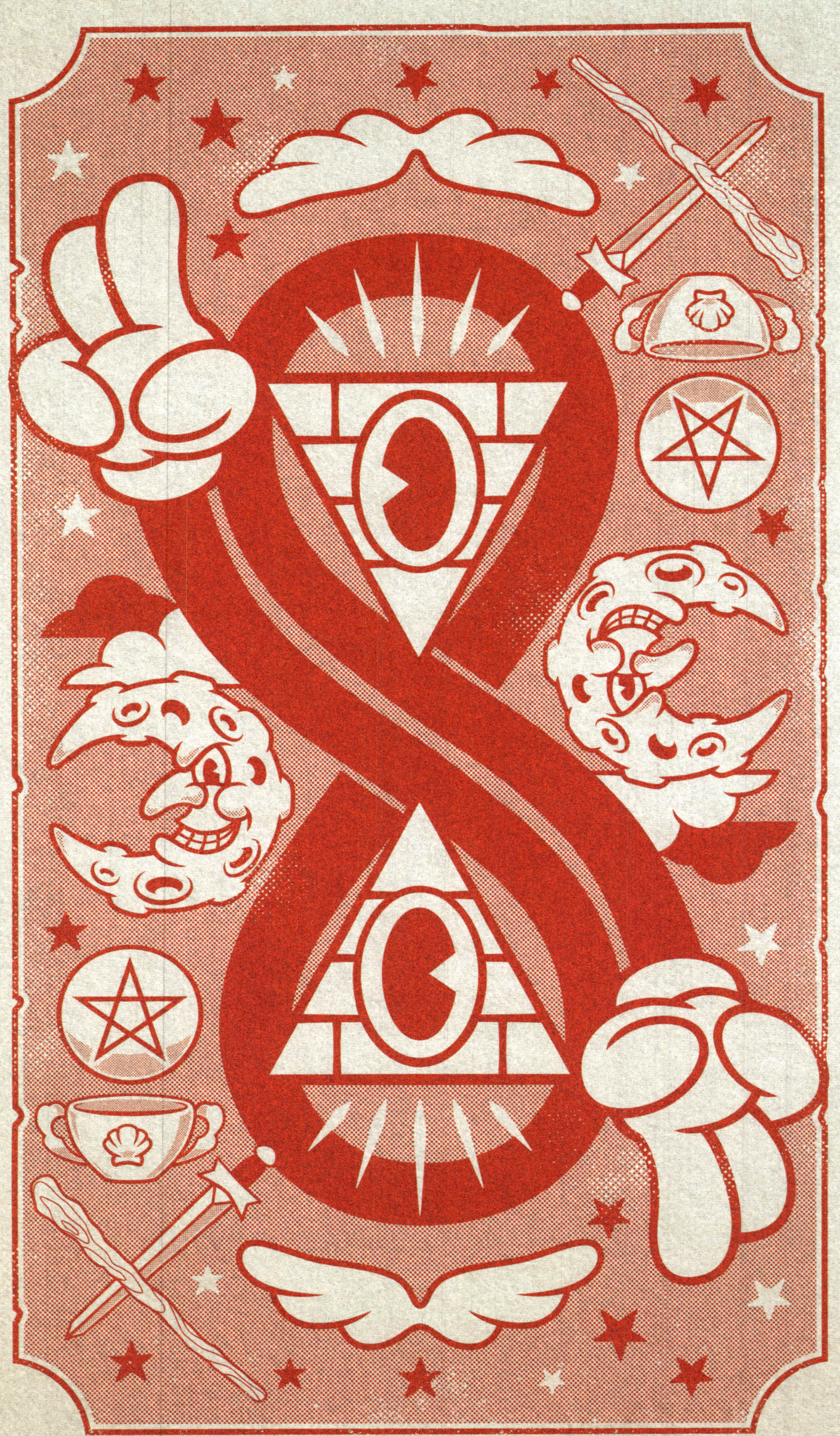

VII

THE CHARIOT

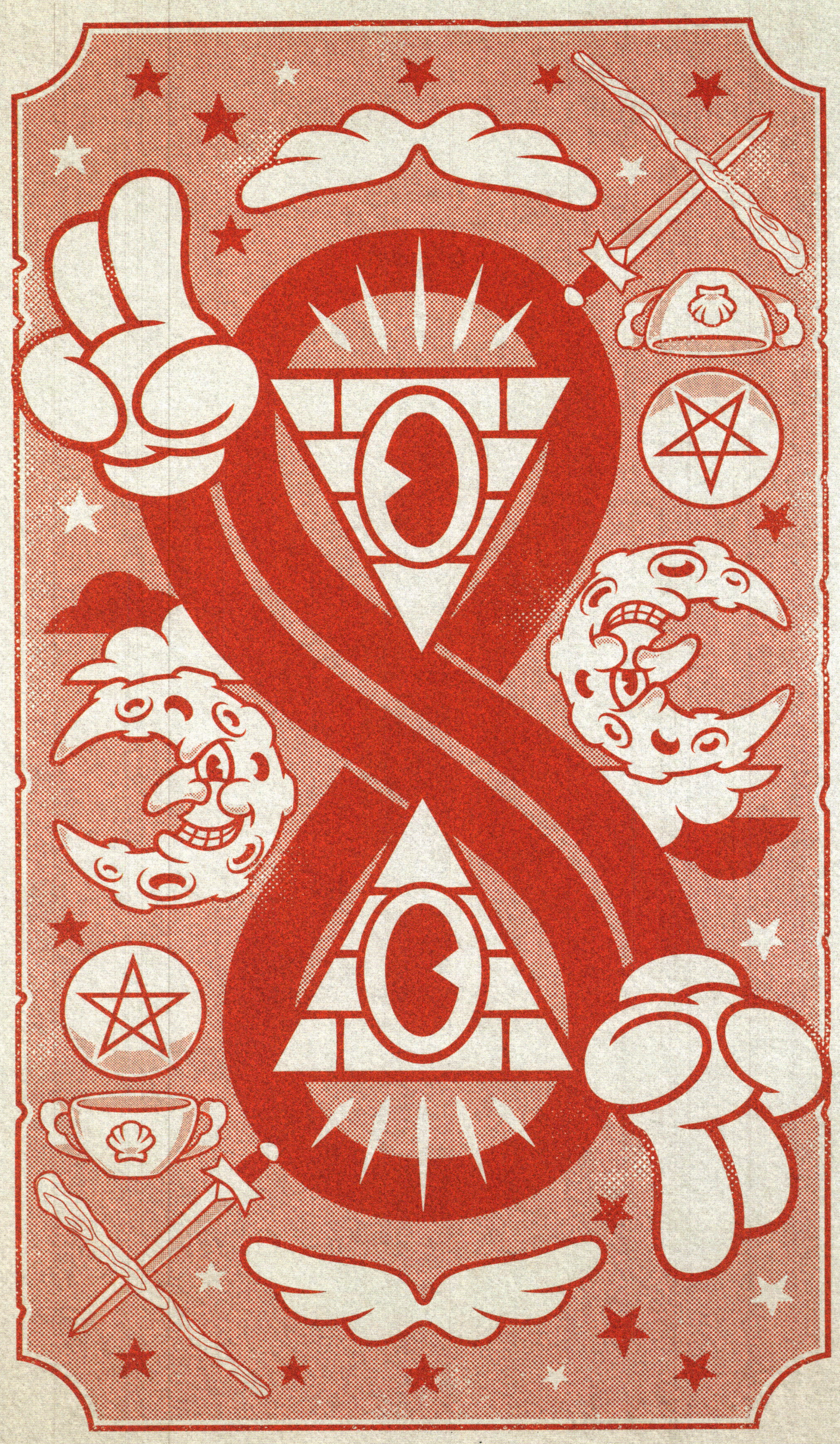

VIII

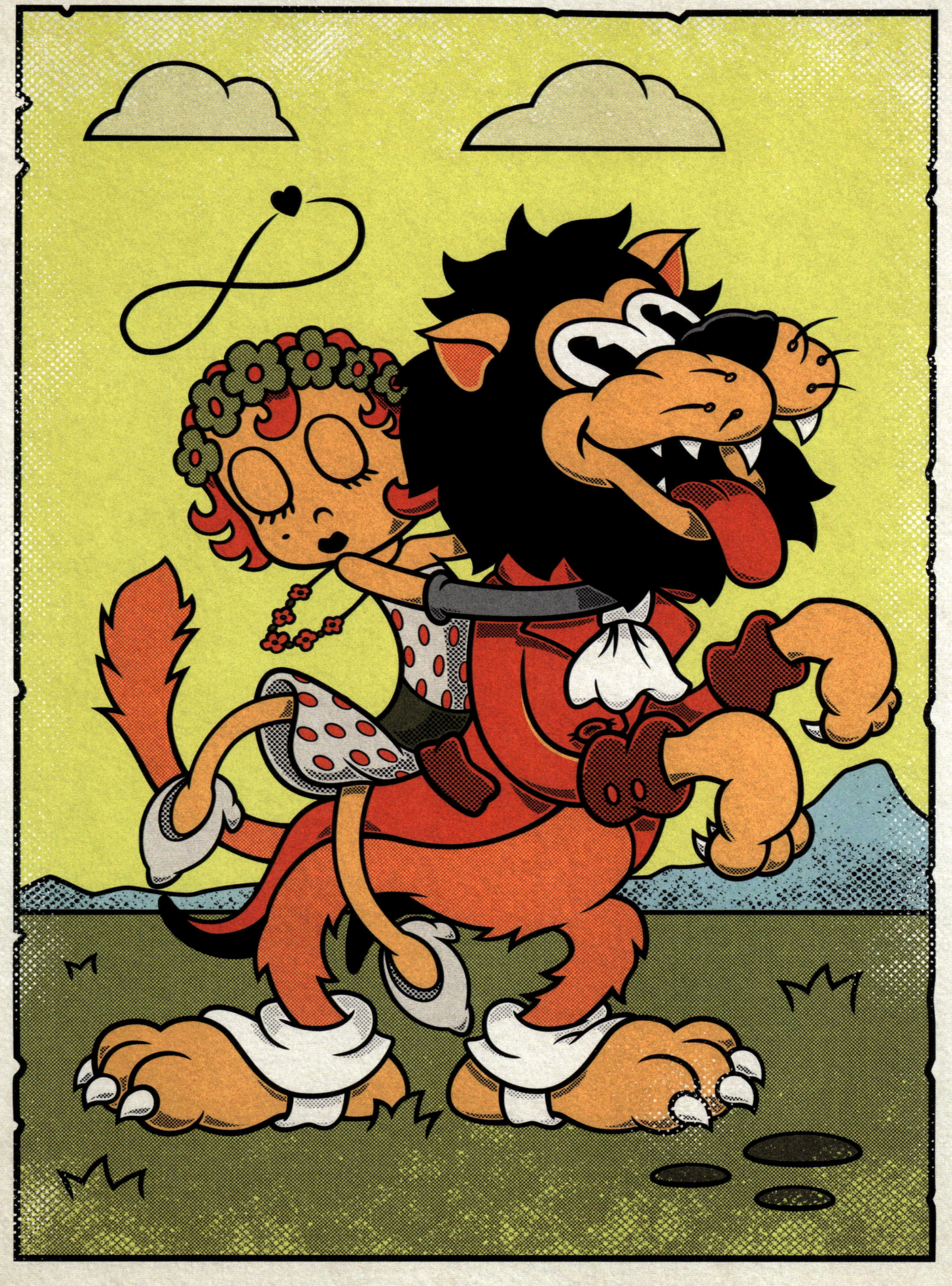

STRENGTH

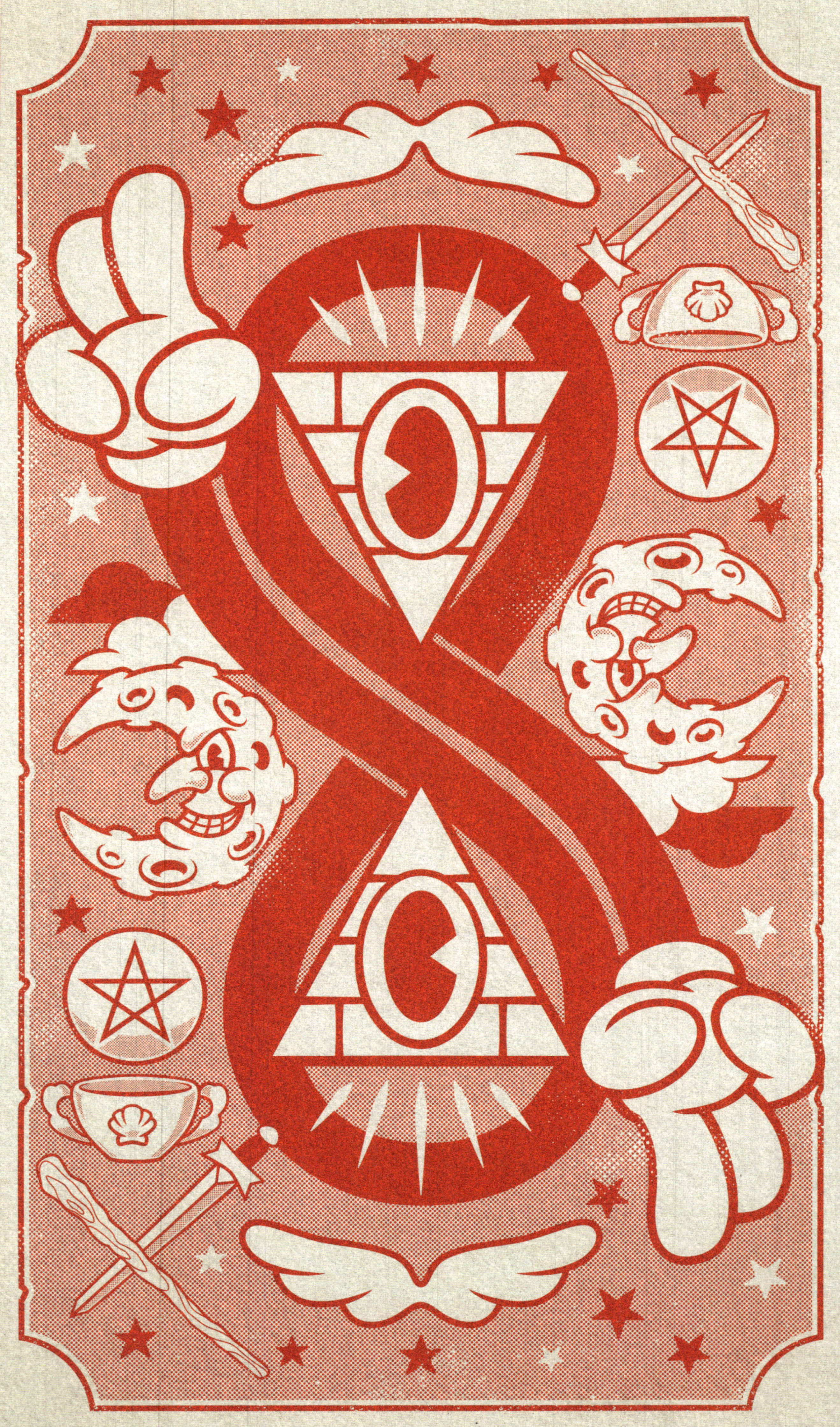

IX

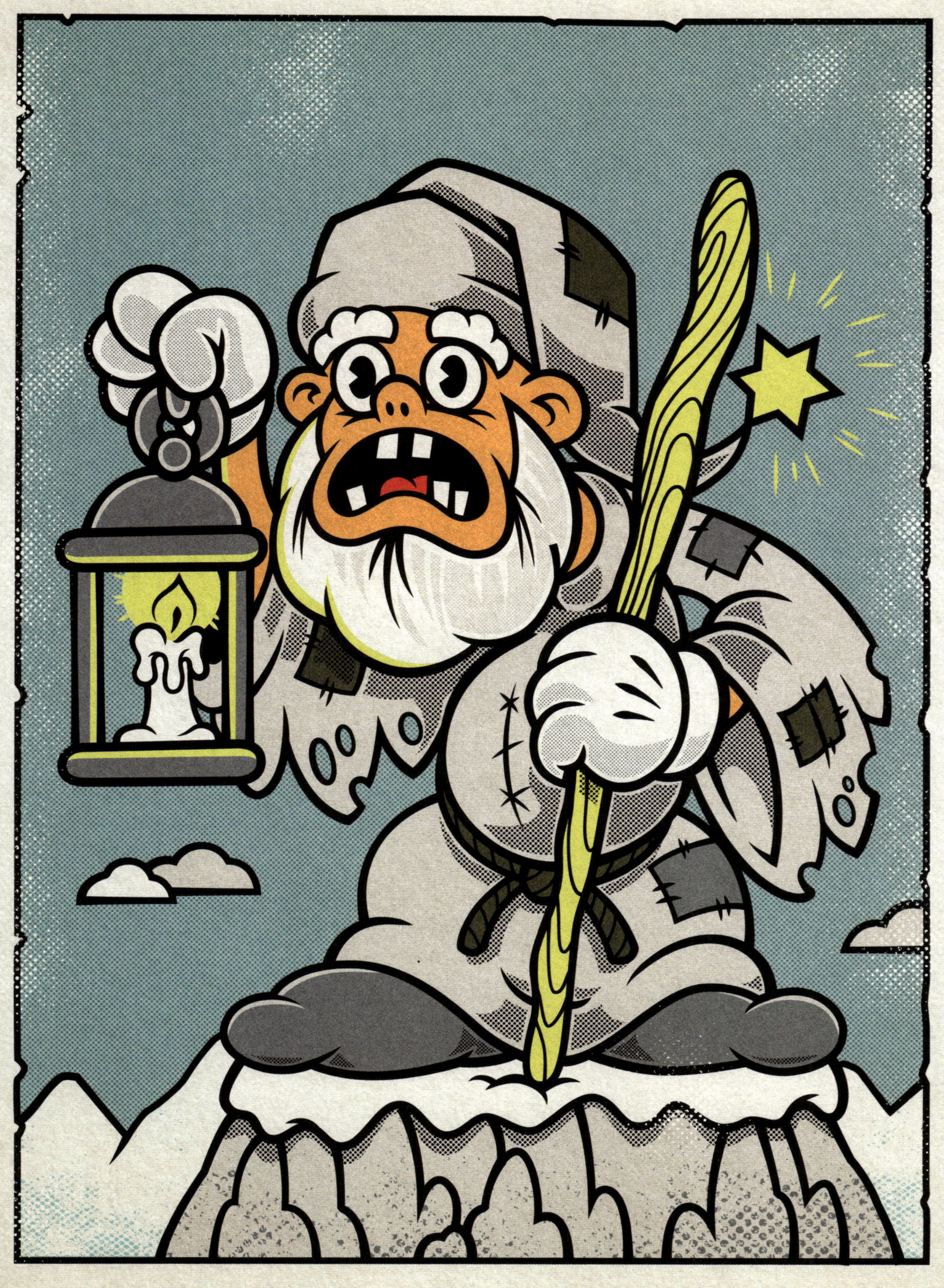

THE HERMIT

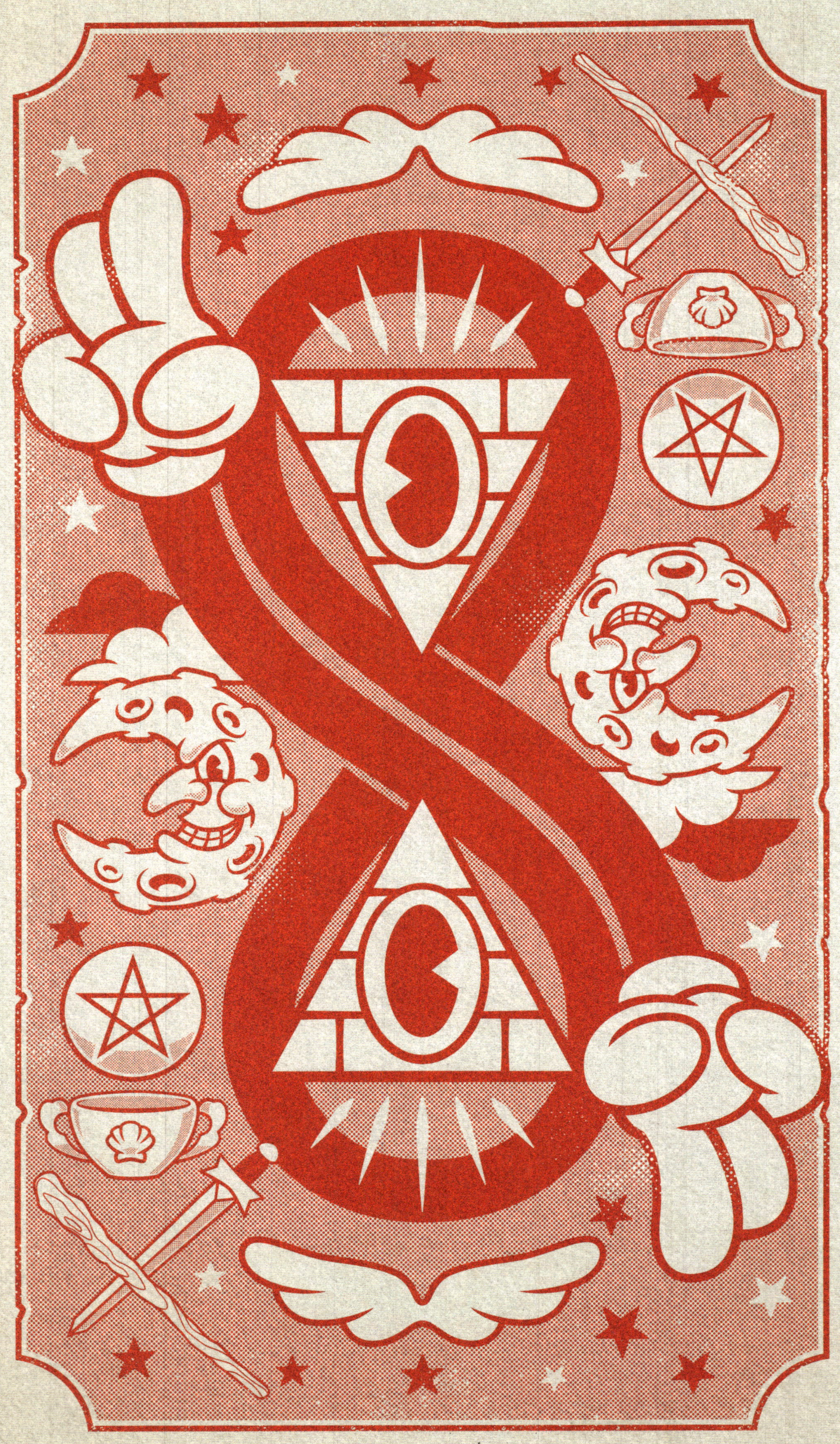

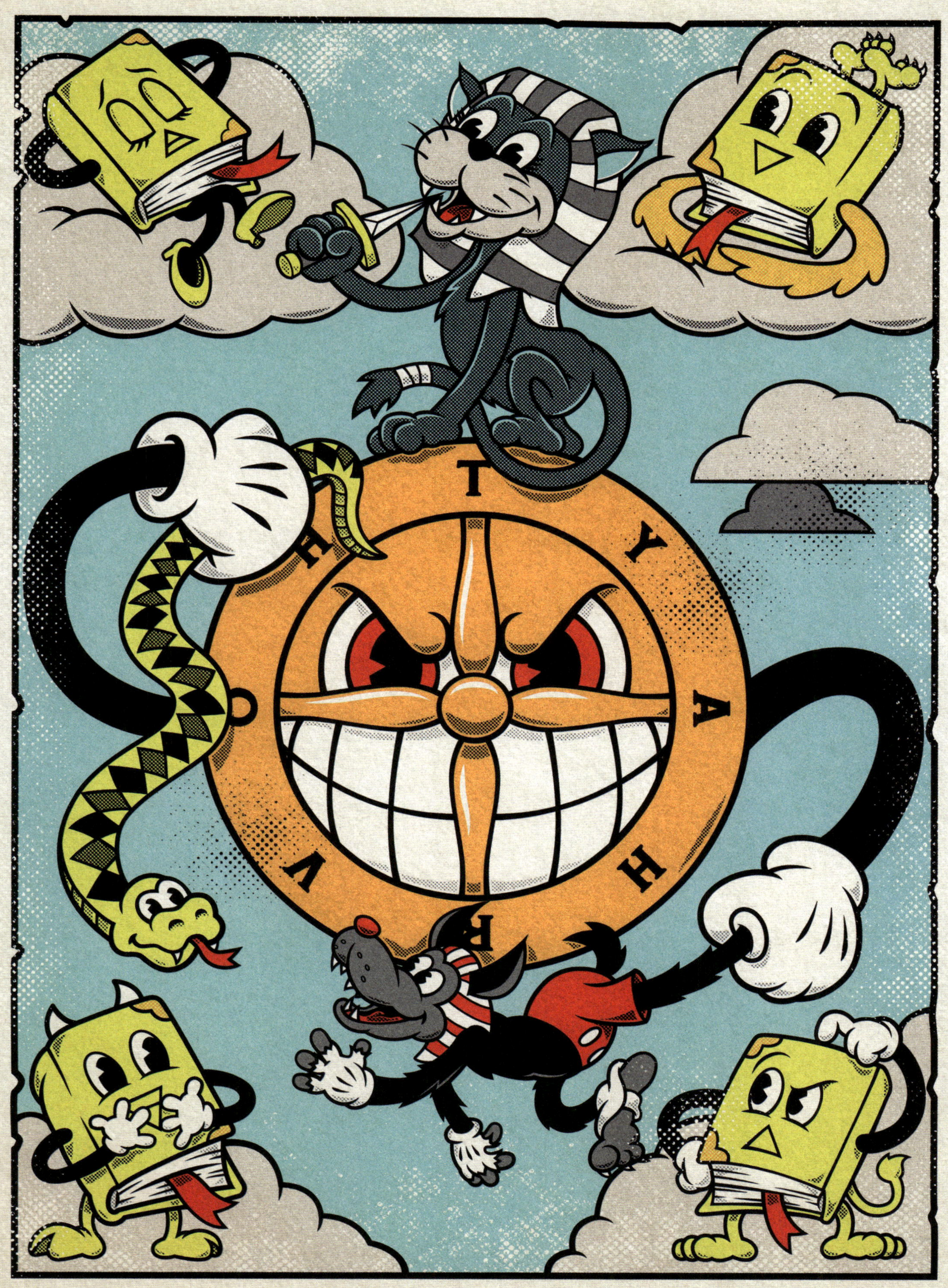

X
WHEEL OF FORTUNE

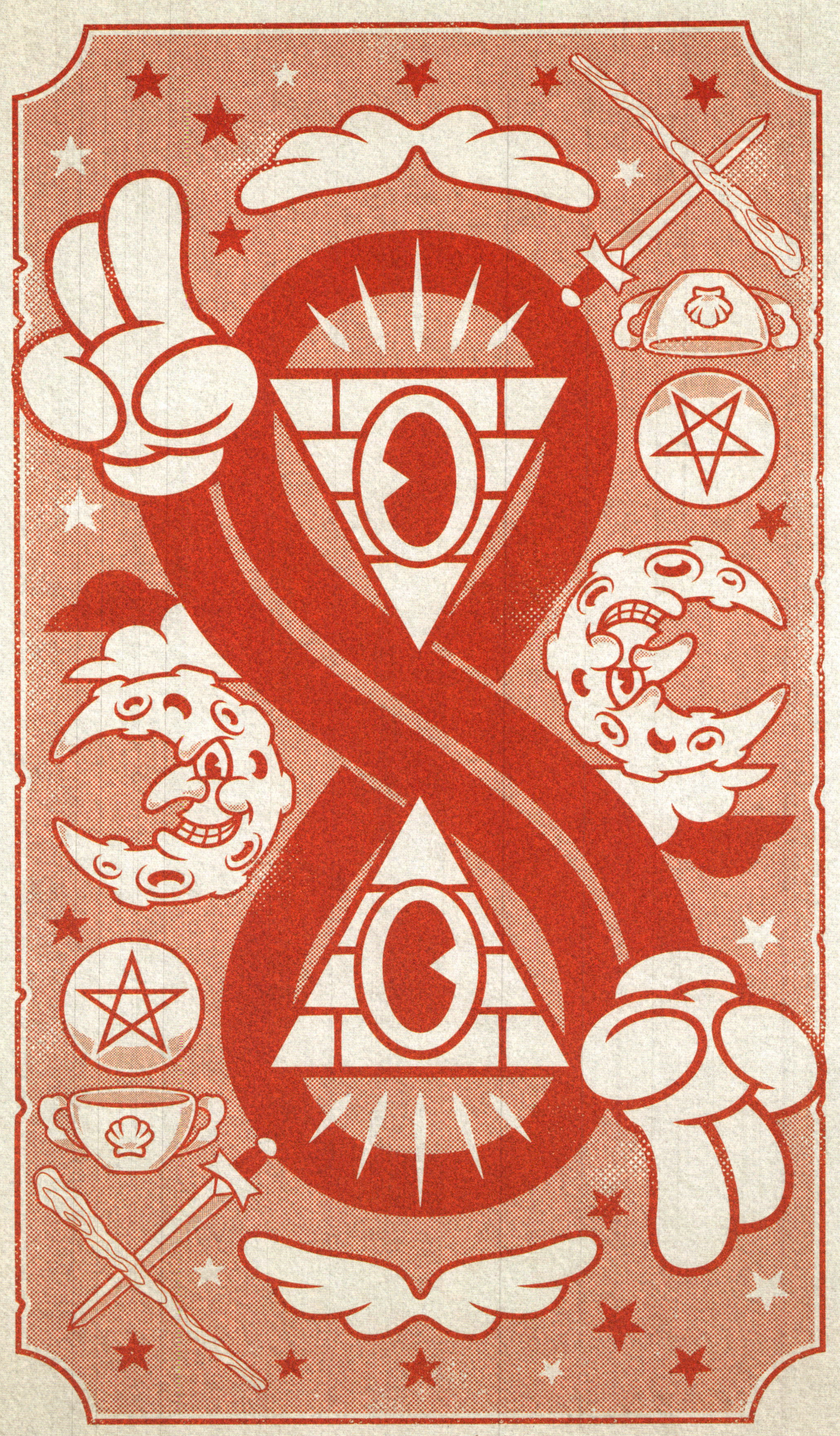

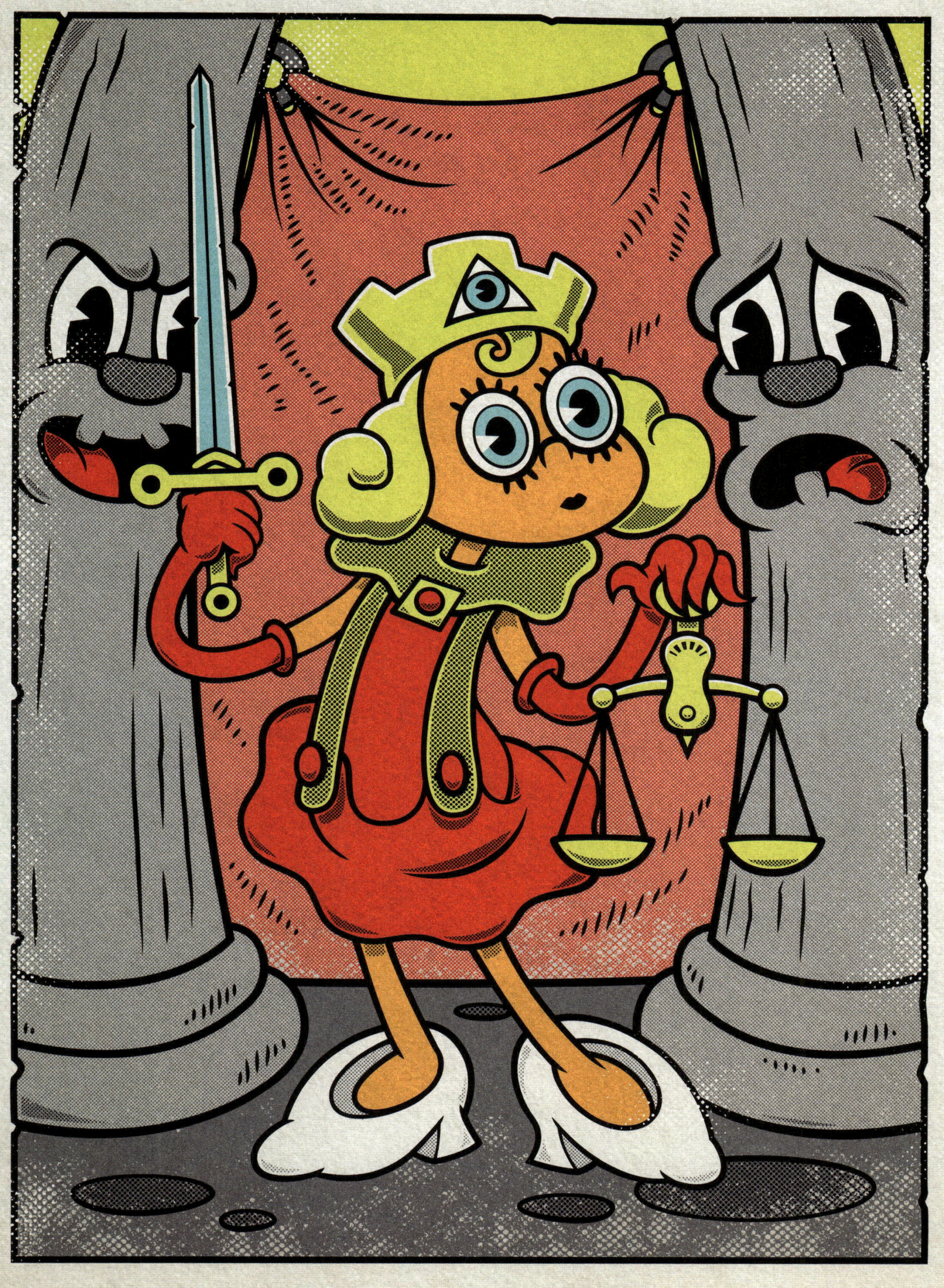

XI
JUSTICE

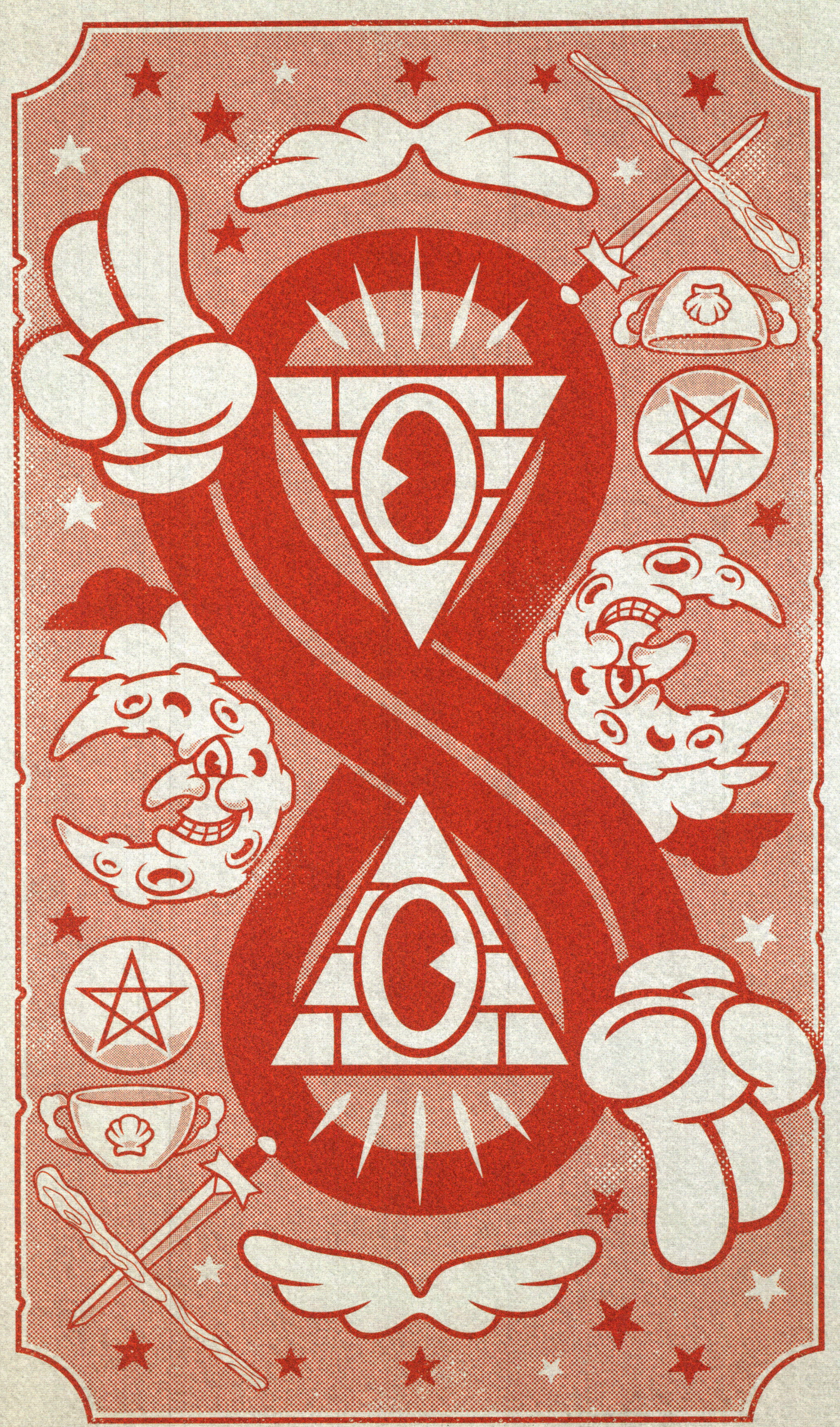

XII

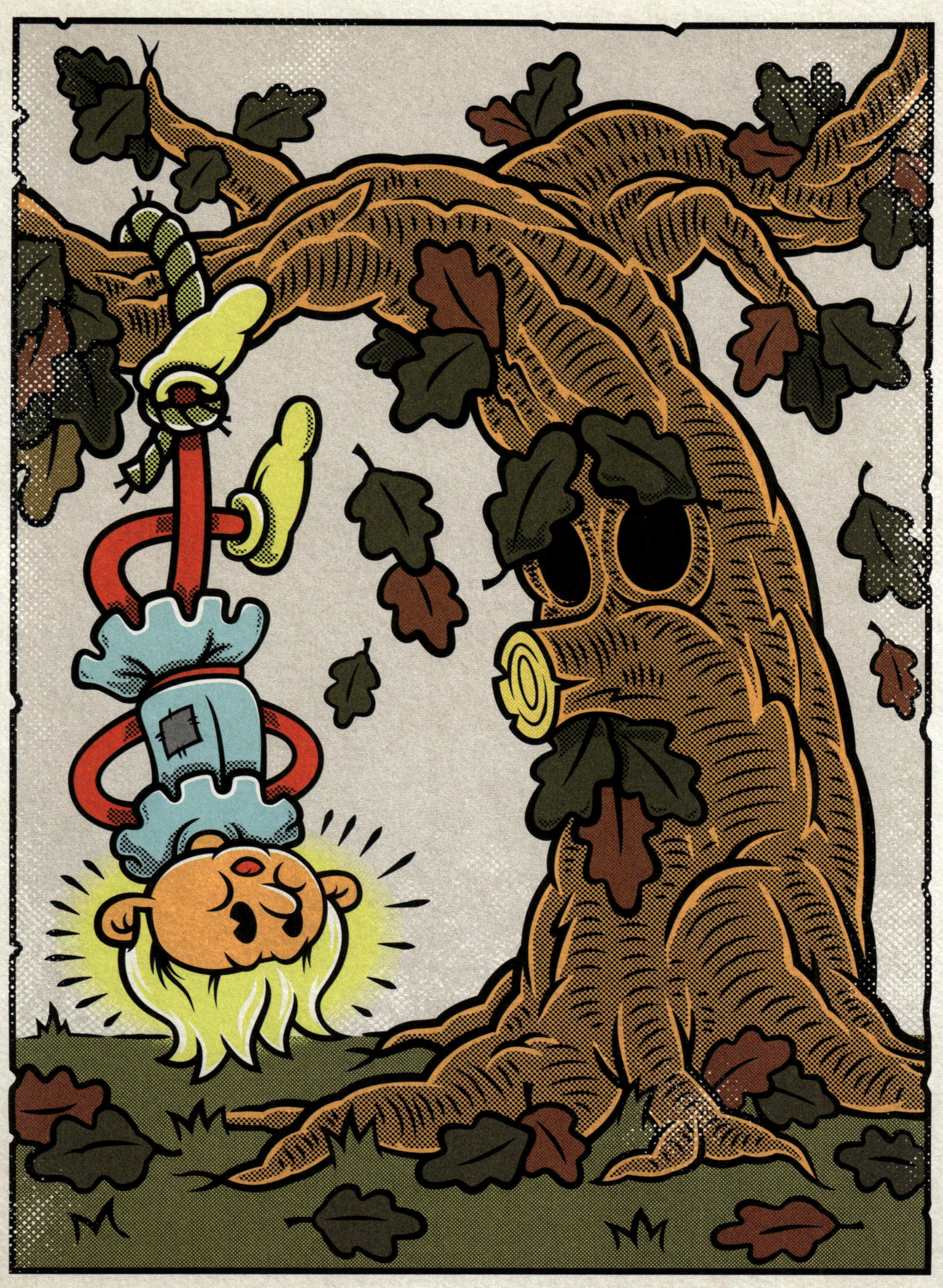

THE HANGED MAN

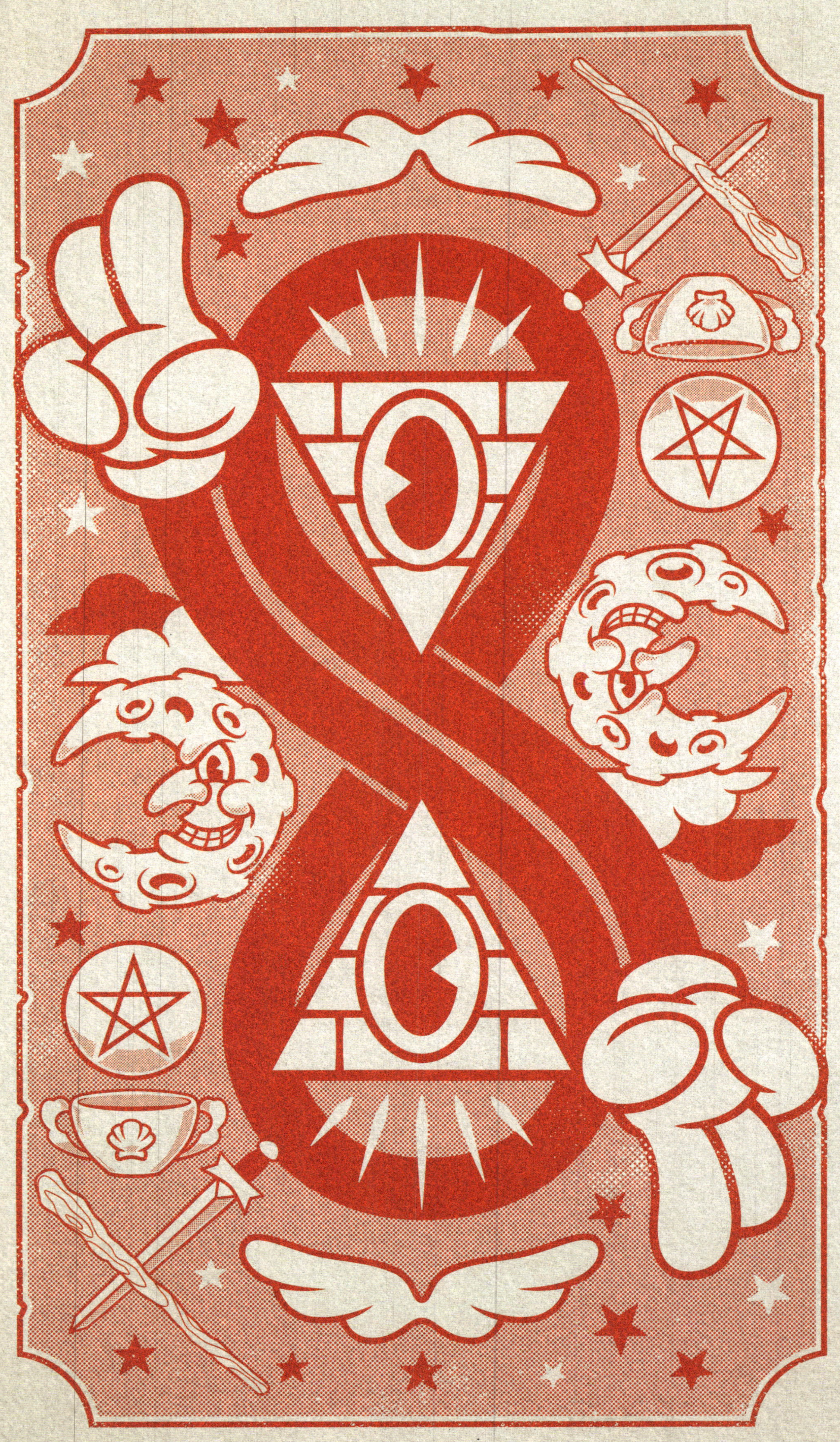

XIII

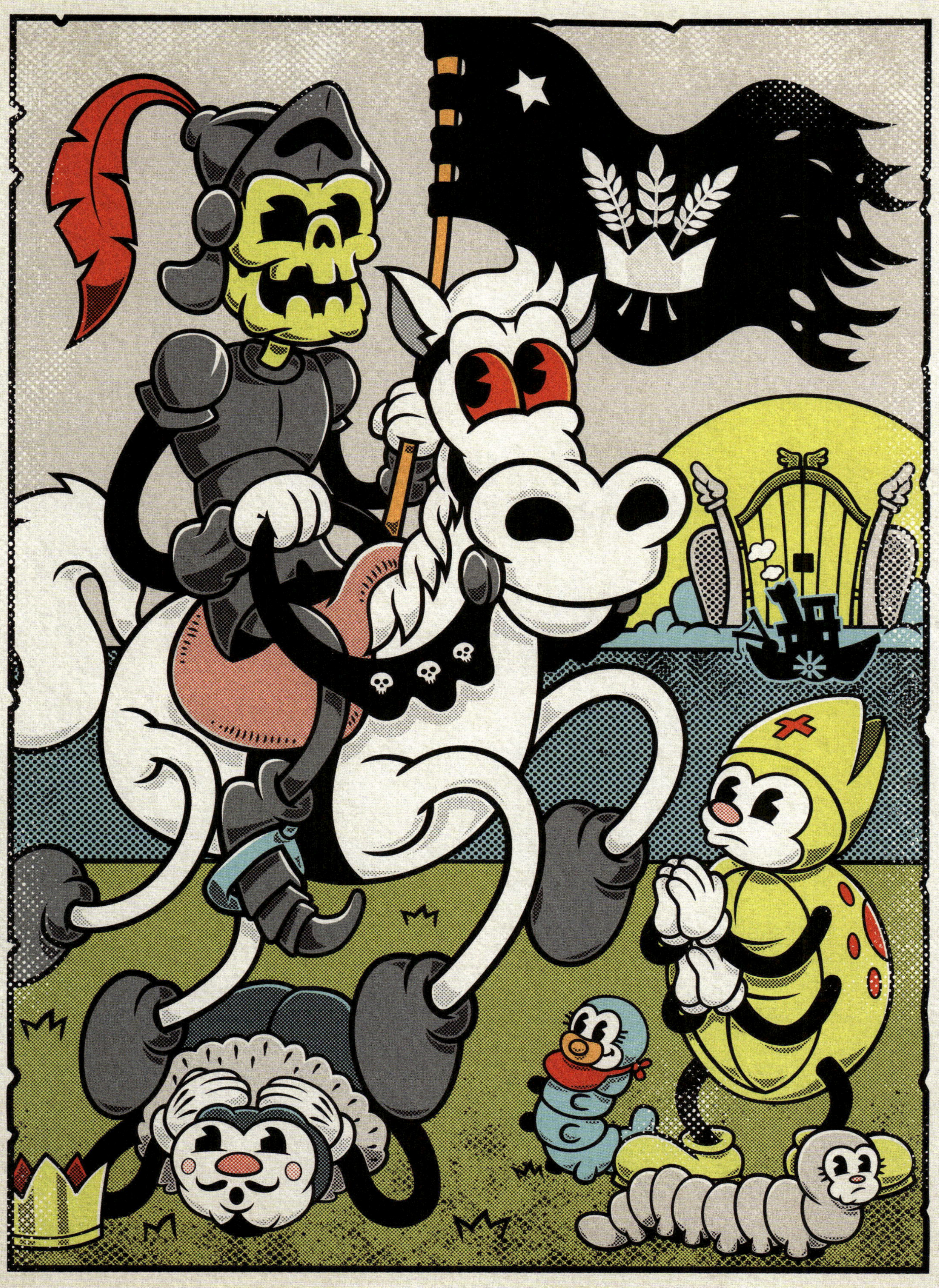

DEATH

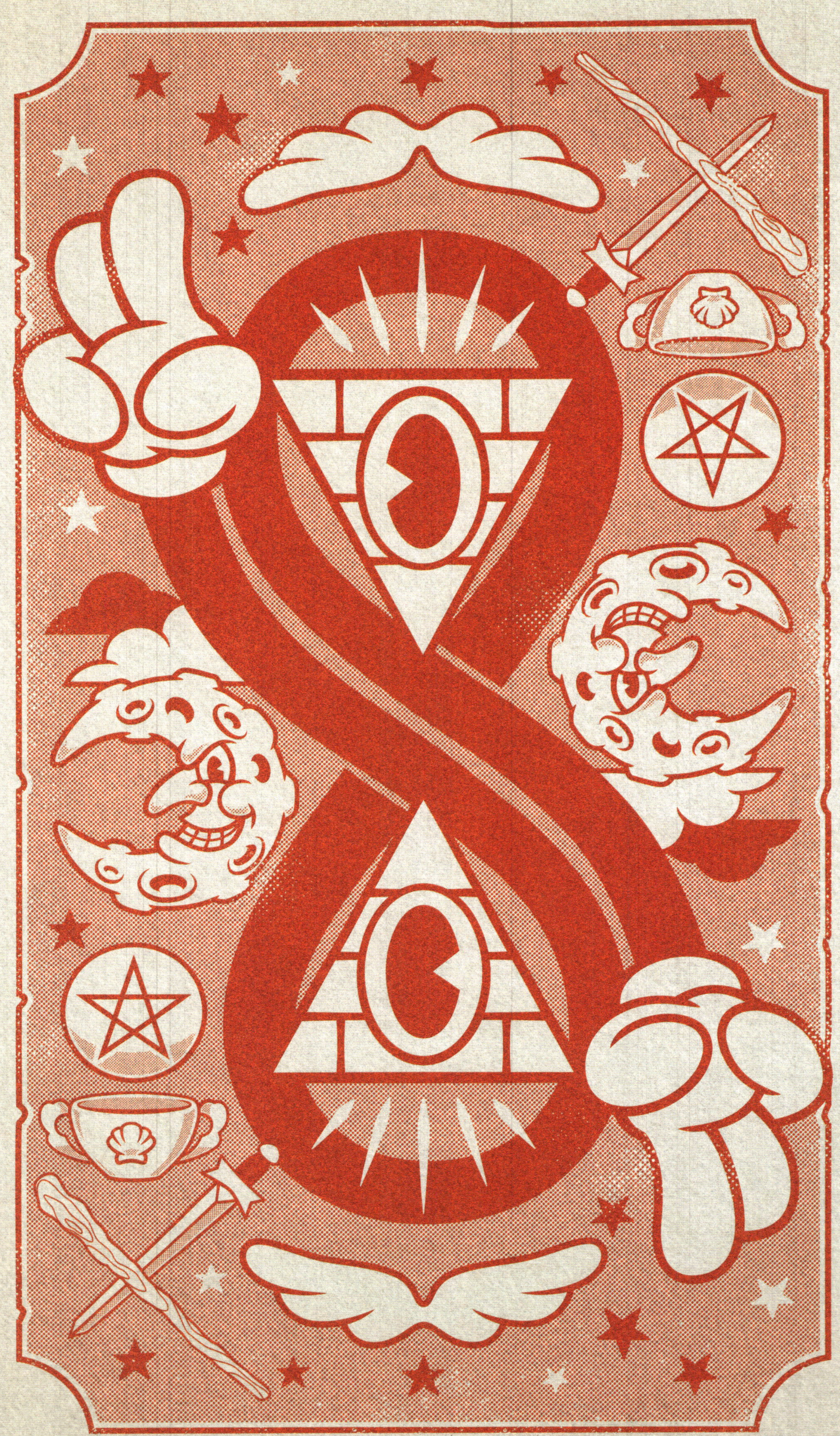

XIV

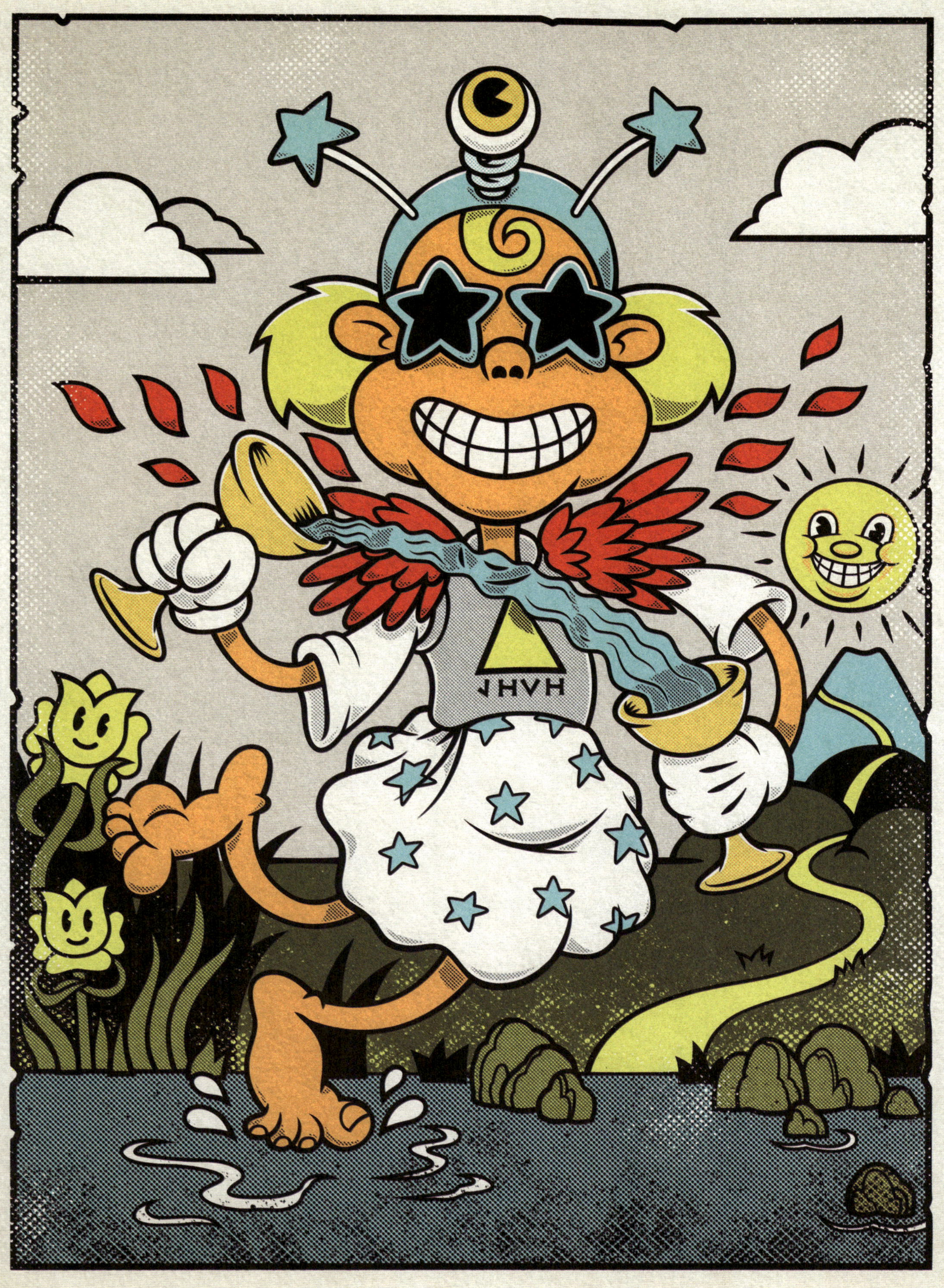

TEMPERANCE

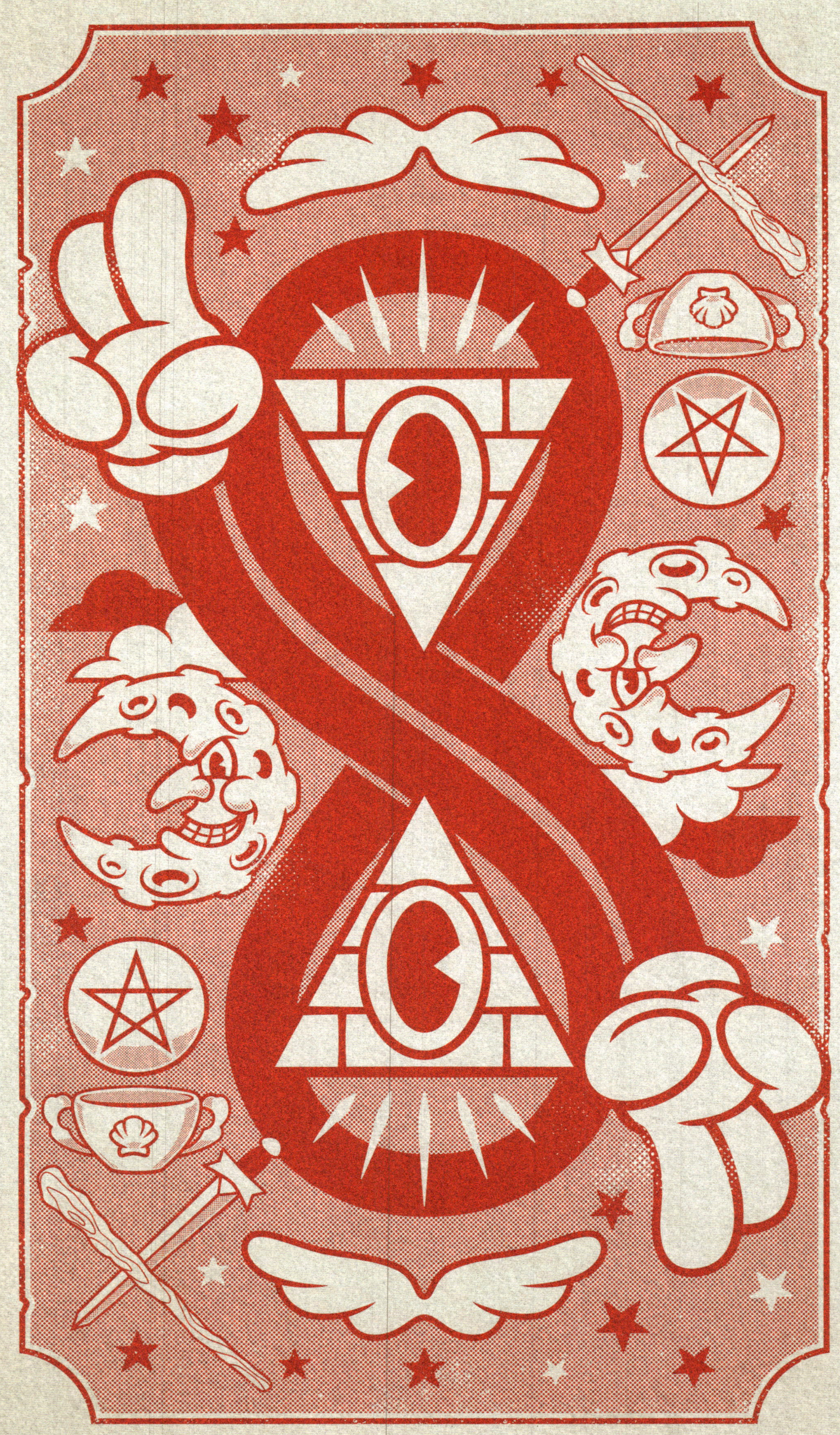

XV

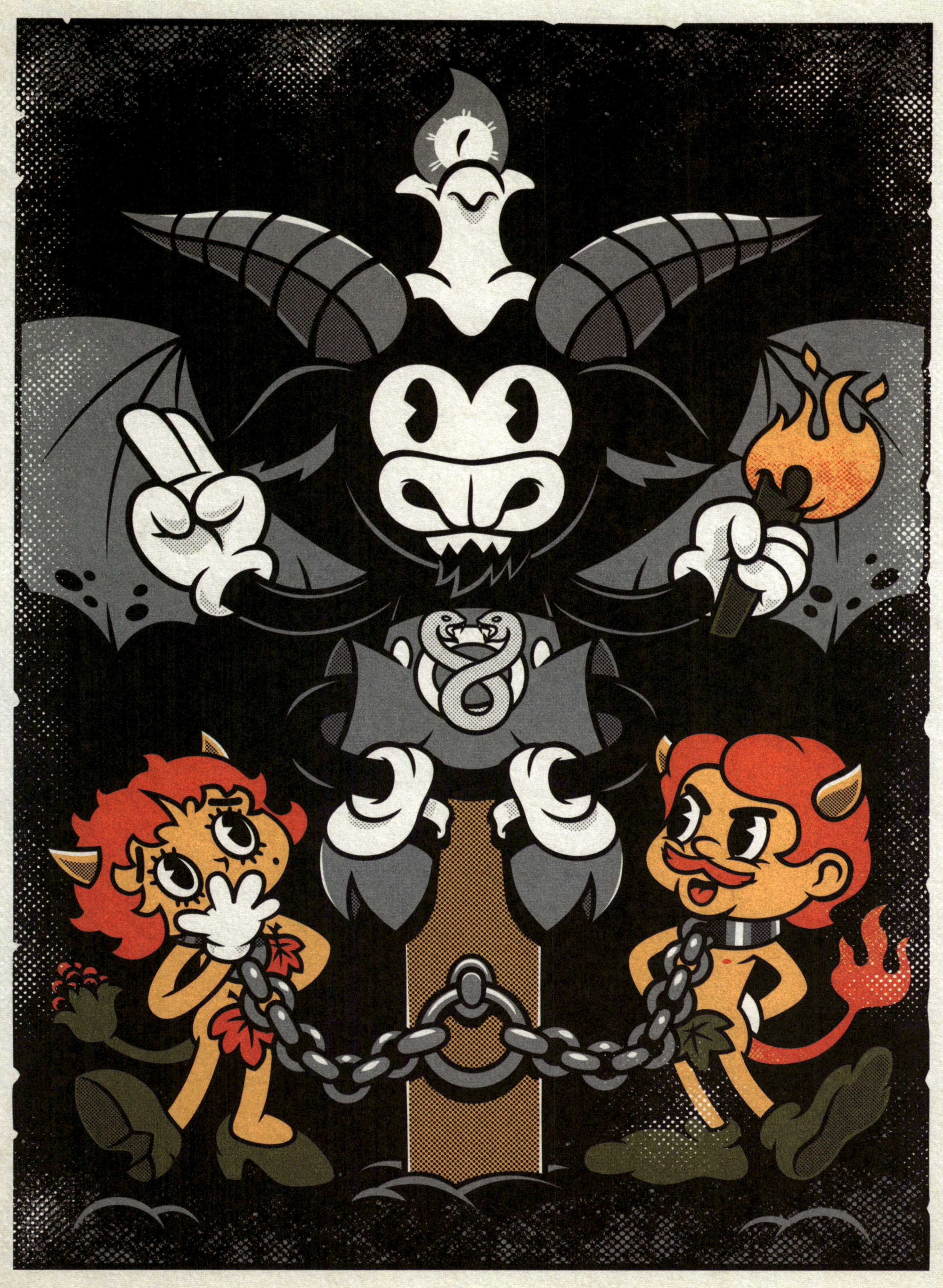

THE DEVIL

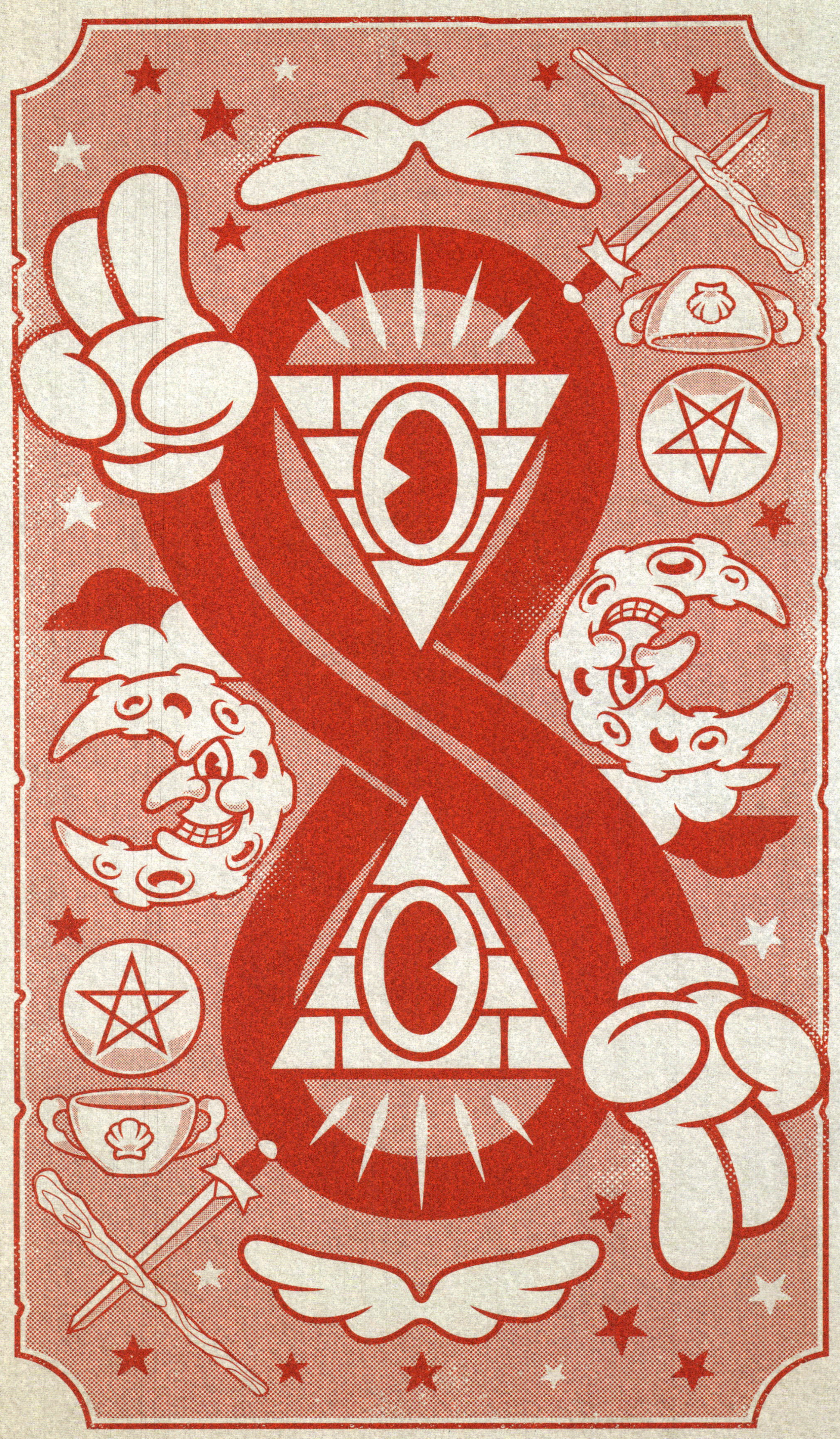

XVI

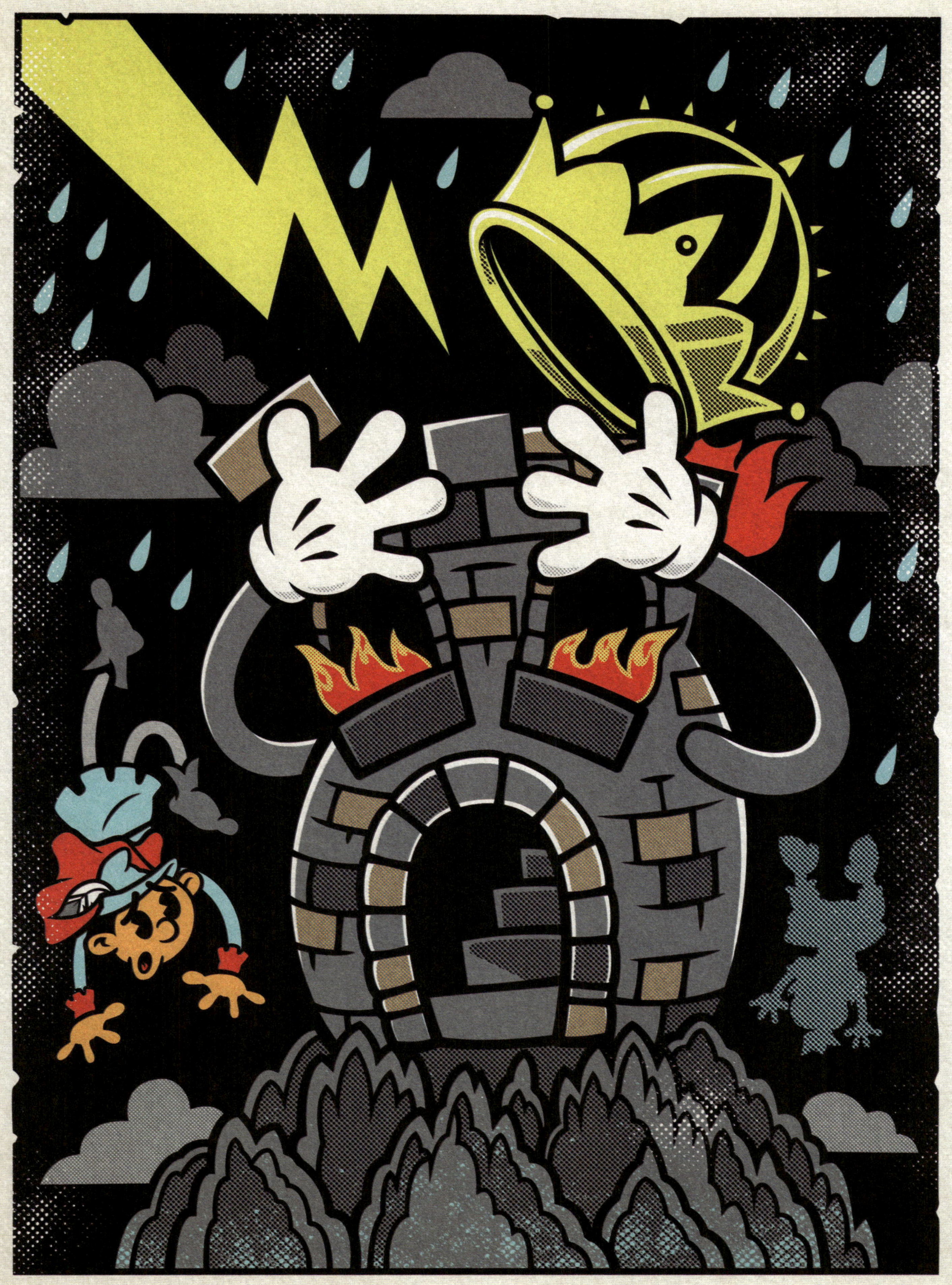

THE TOWER

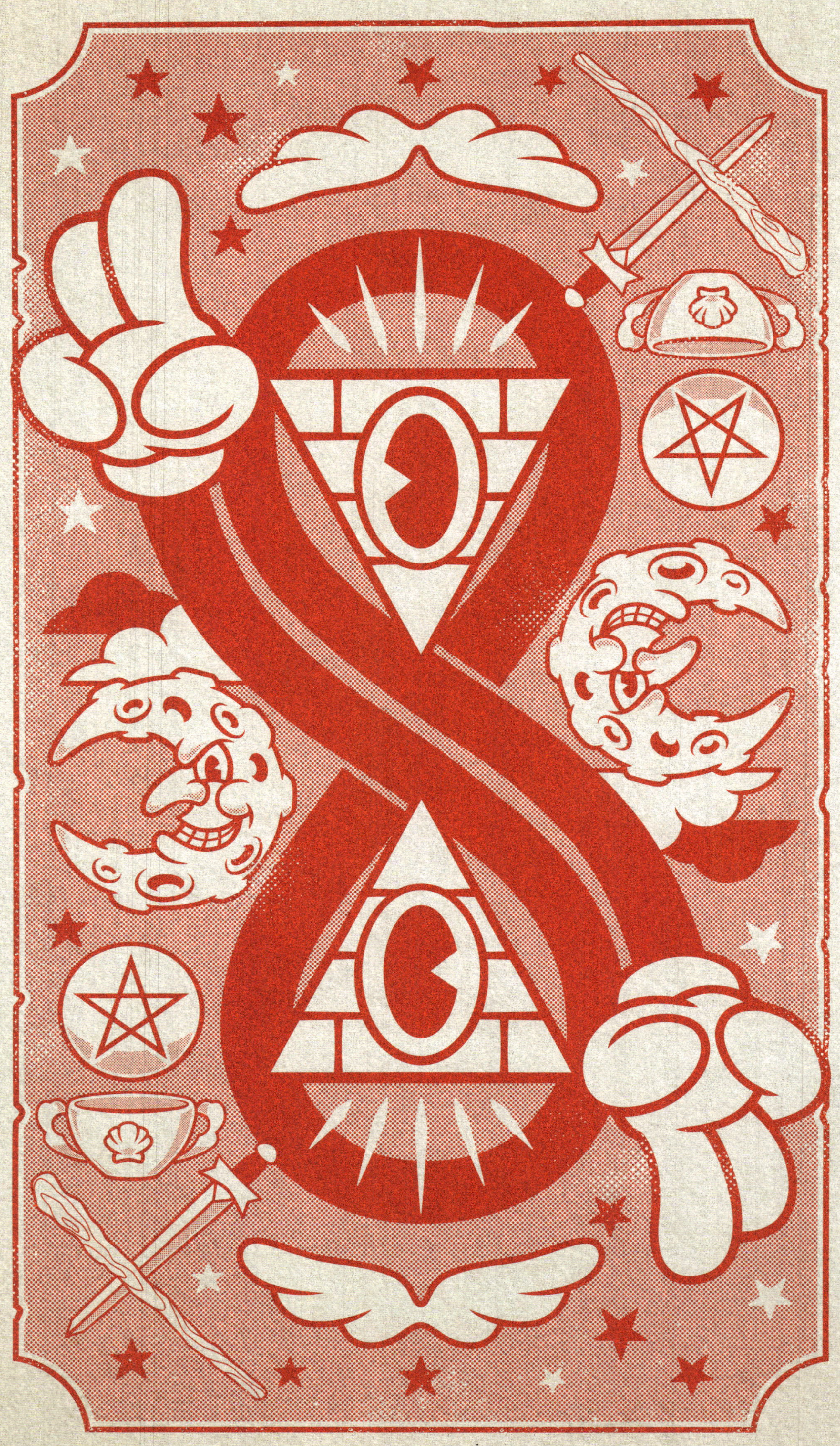

XVII

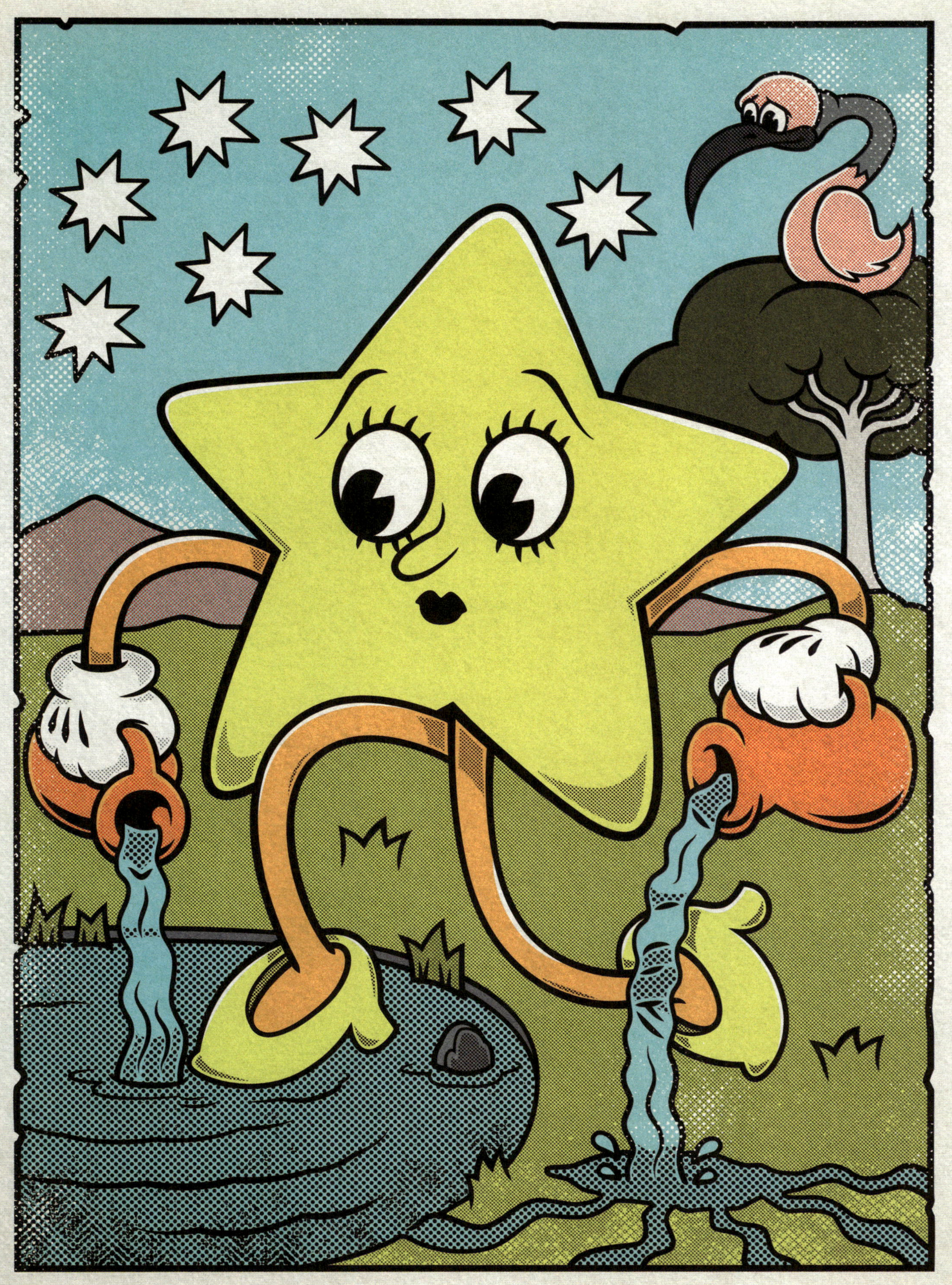

THE STAR

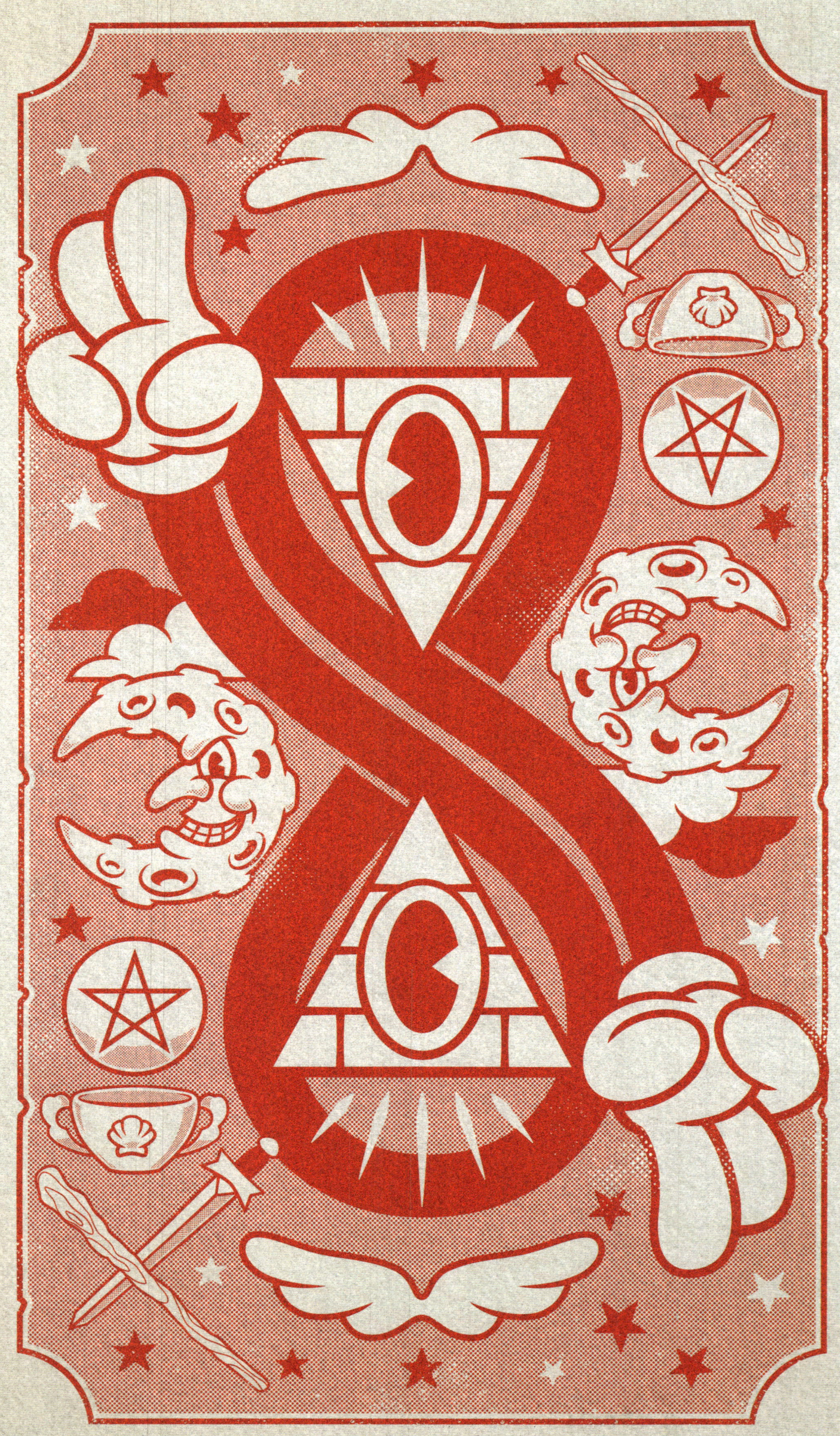

XVIII

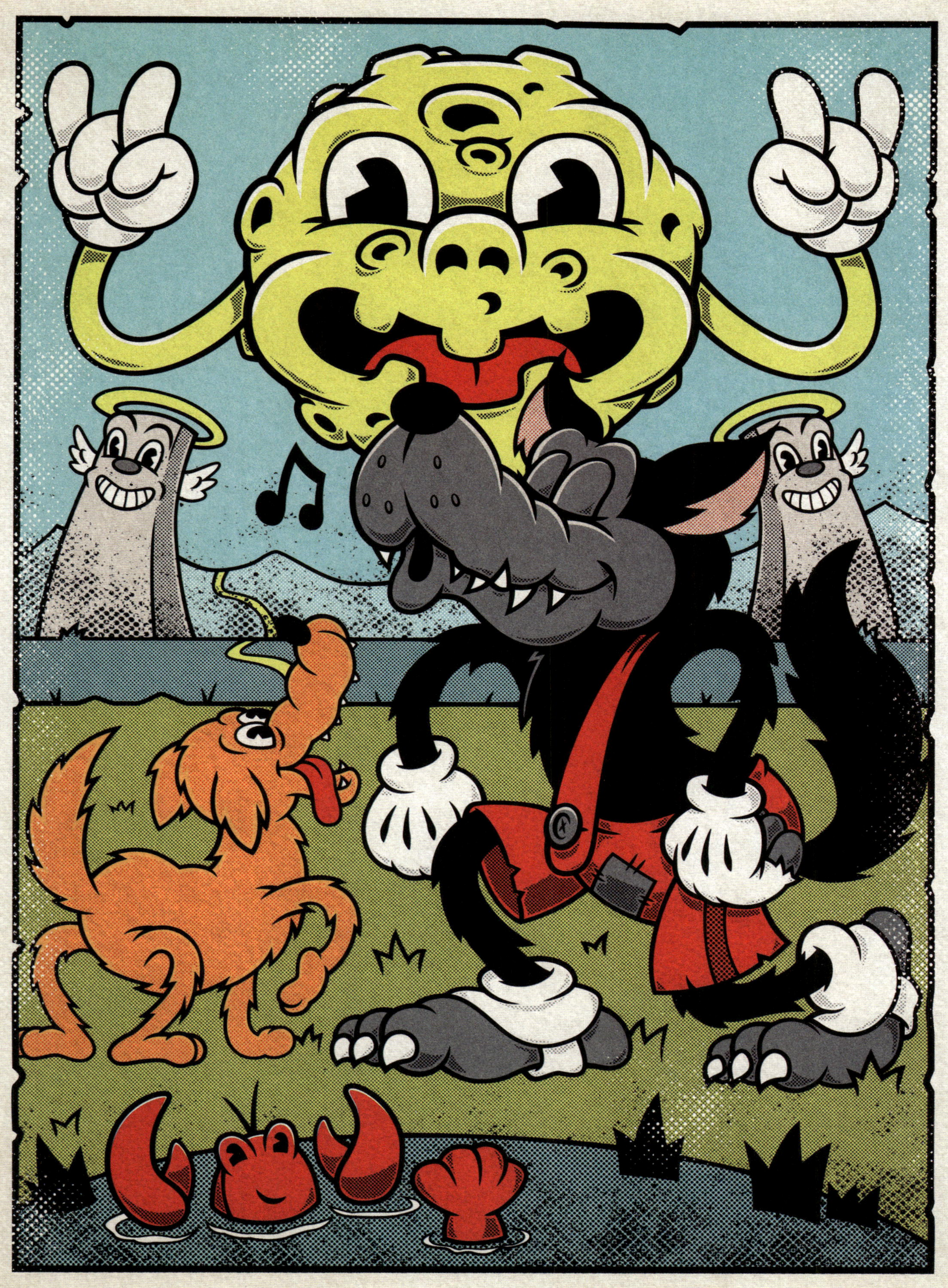

THE MOON

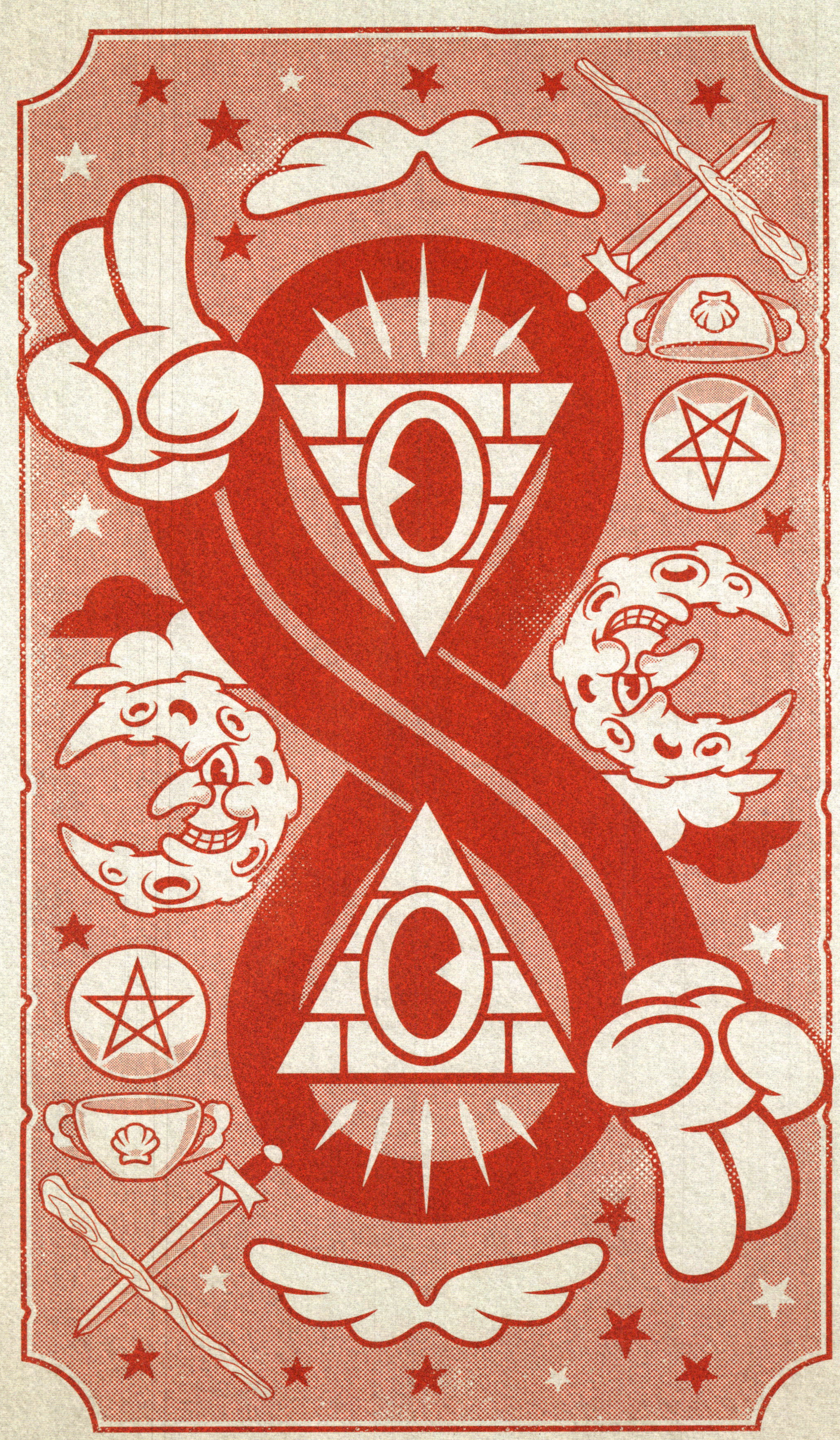

XIX

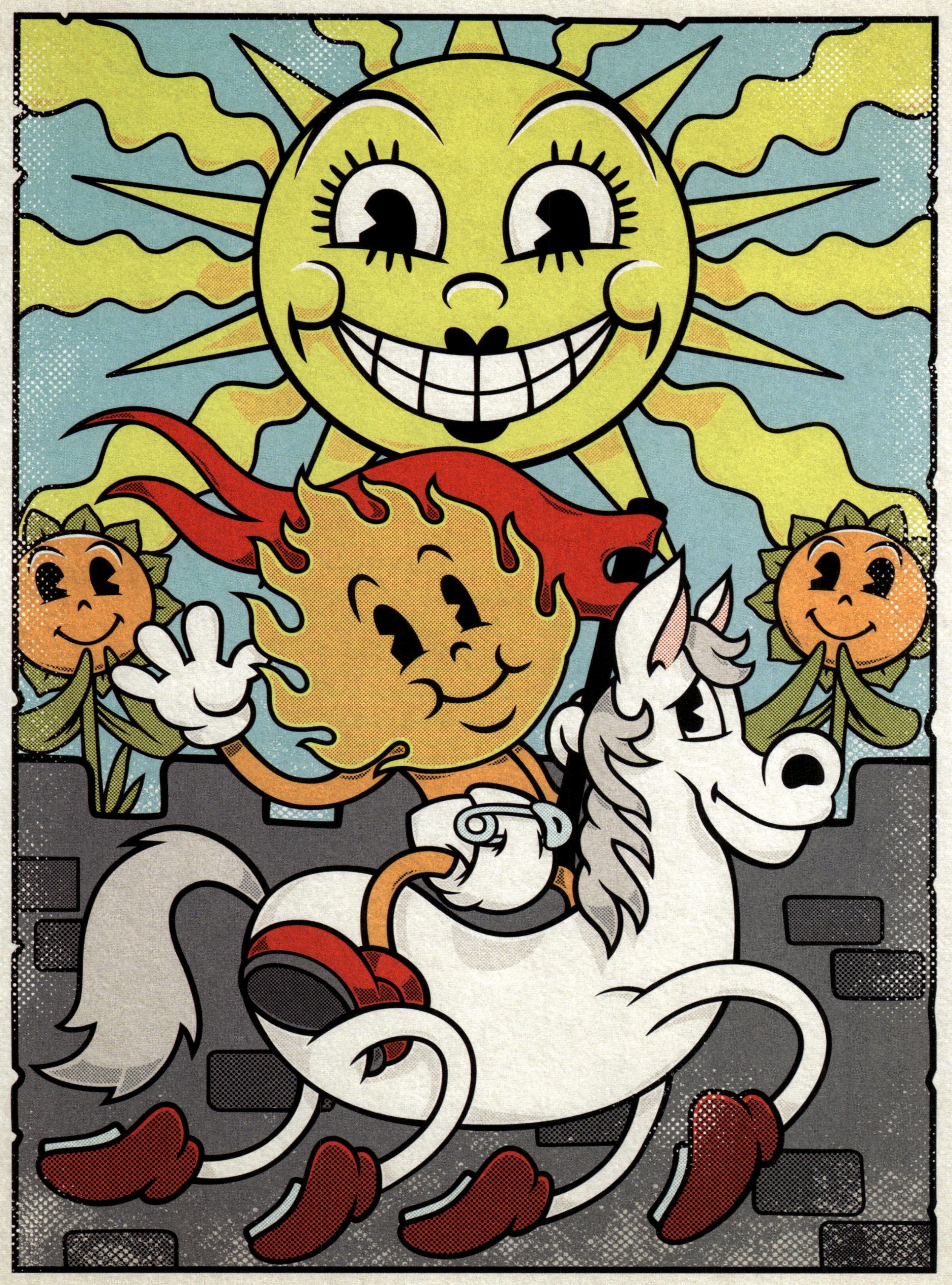

THE SUN

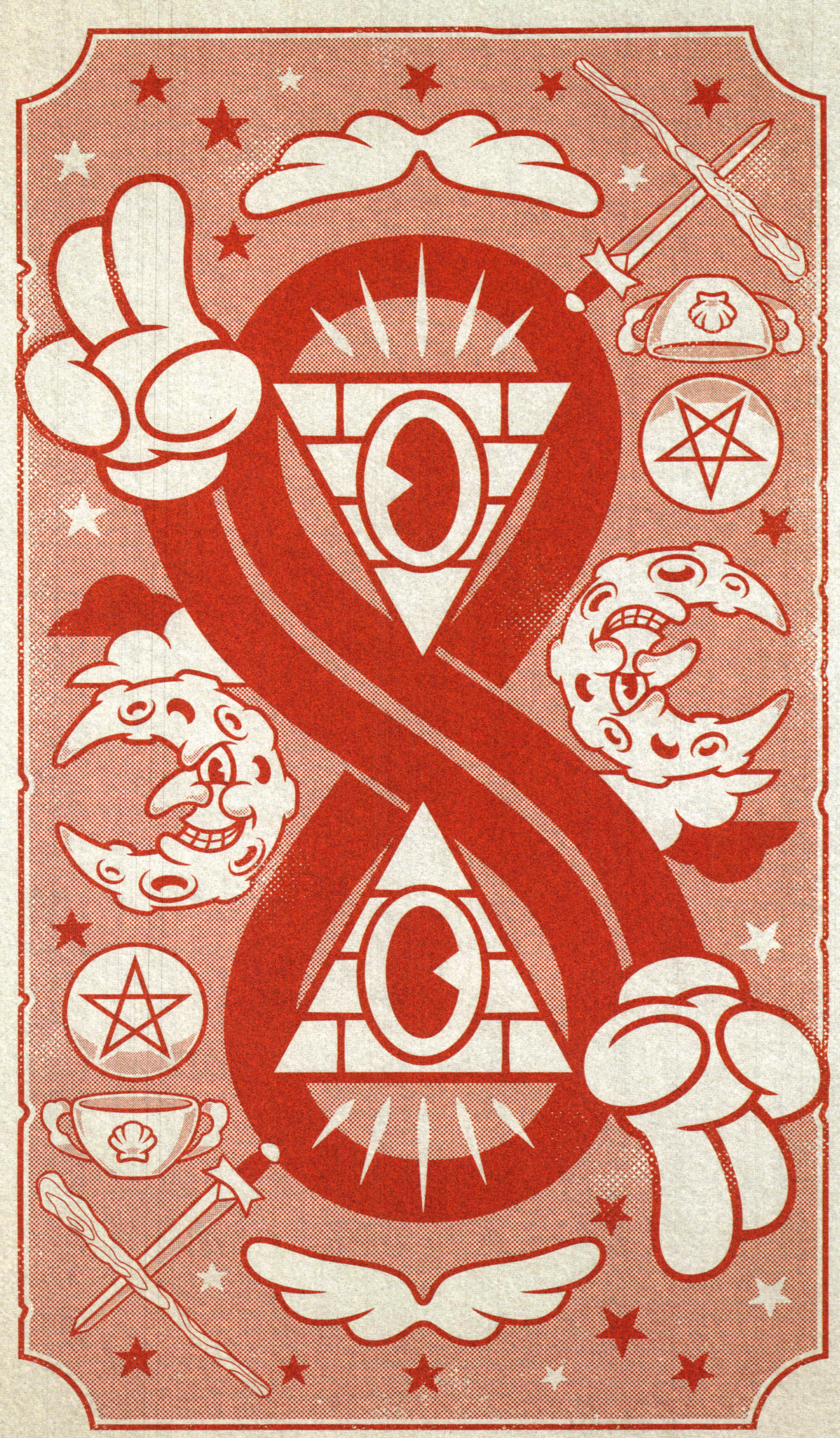

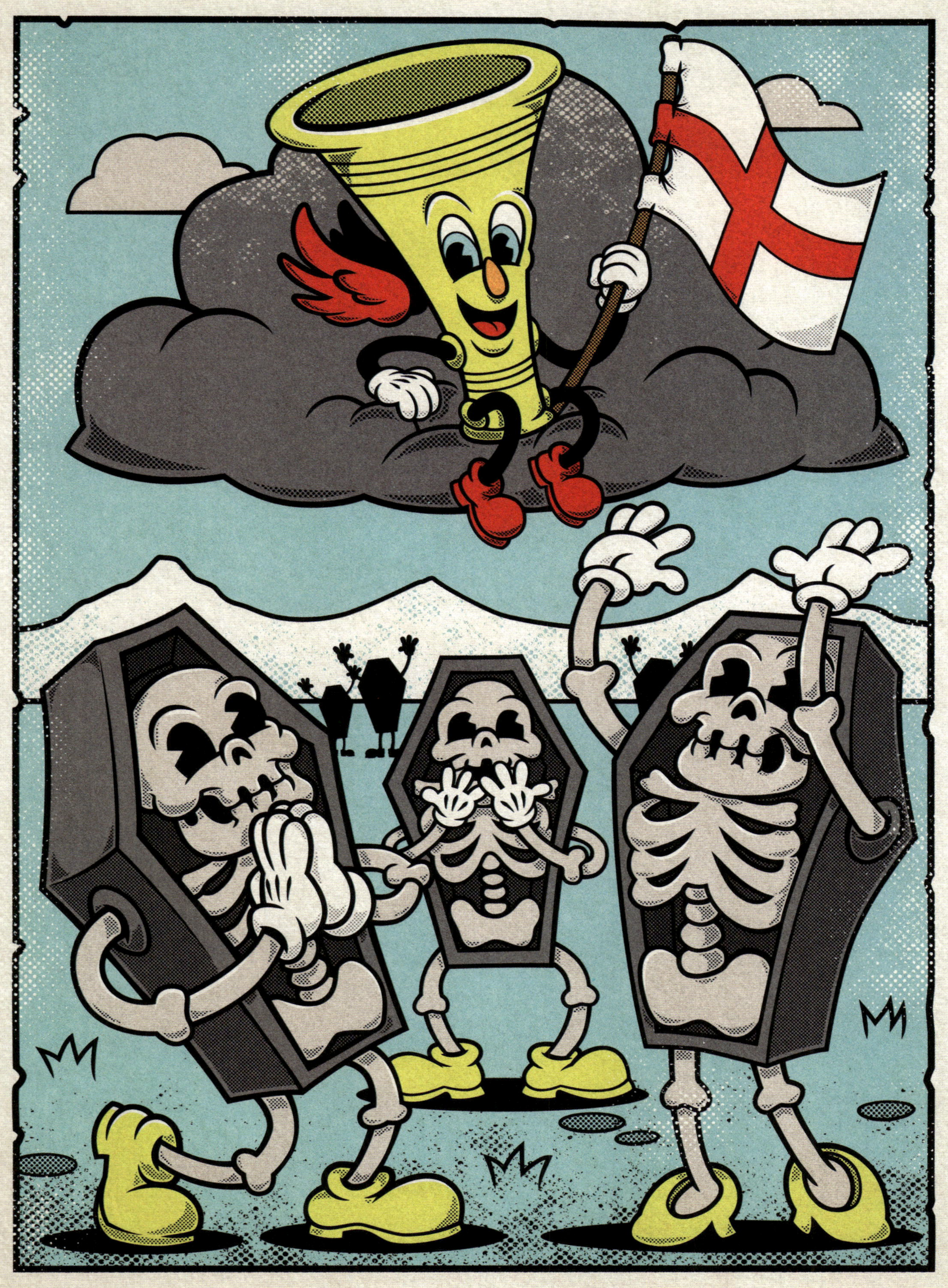

XX
JUDGEMENT

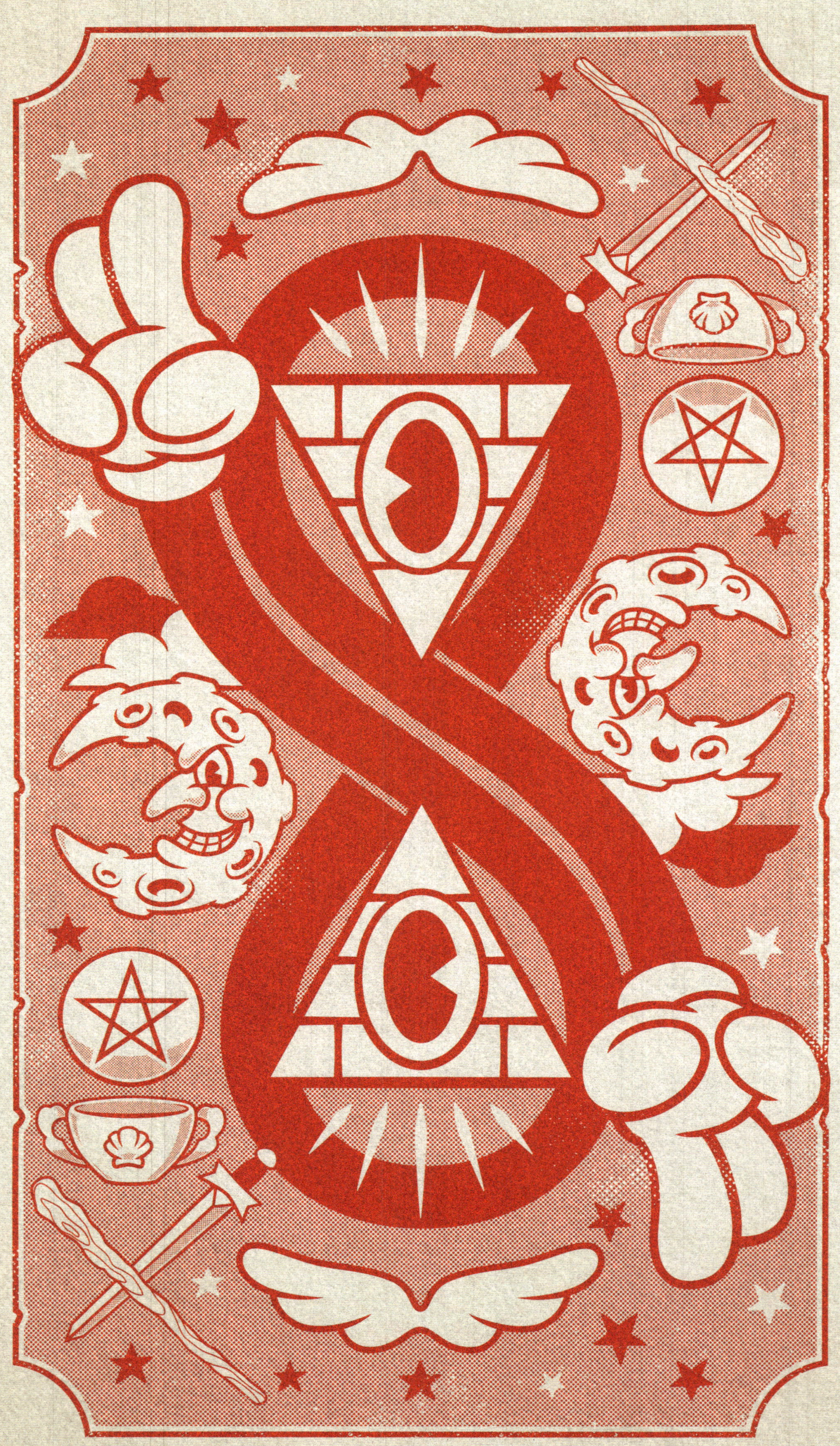

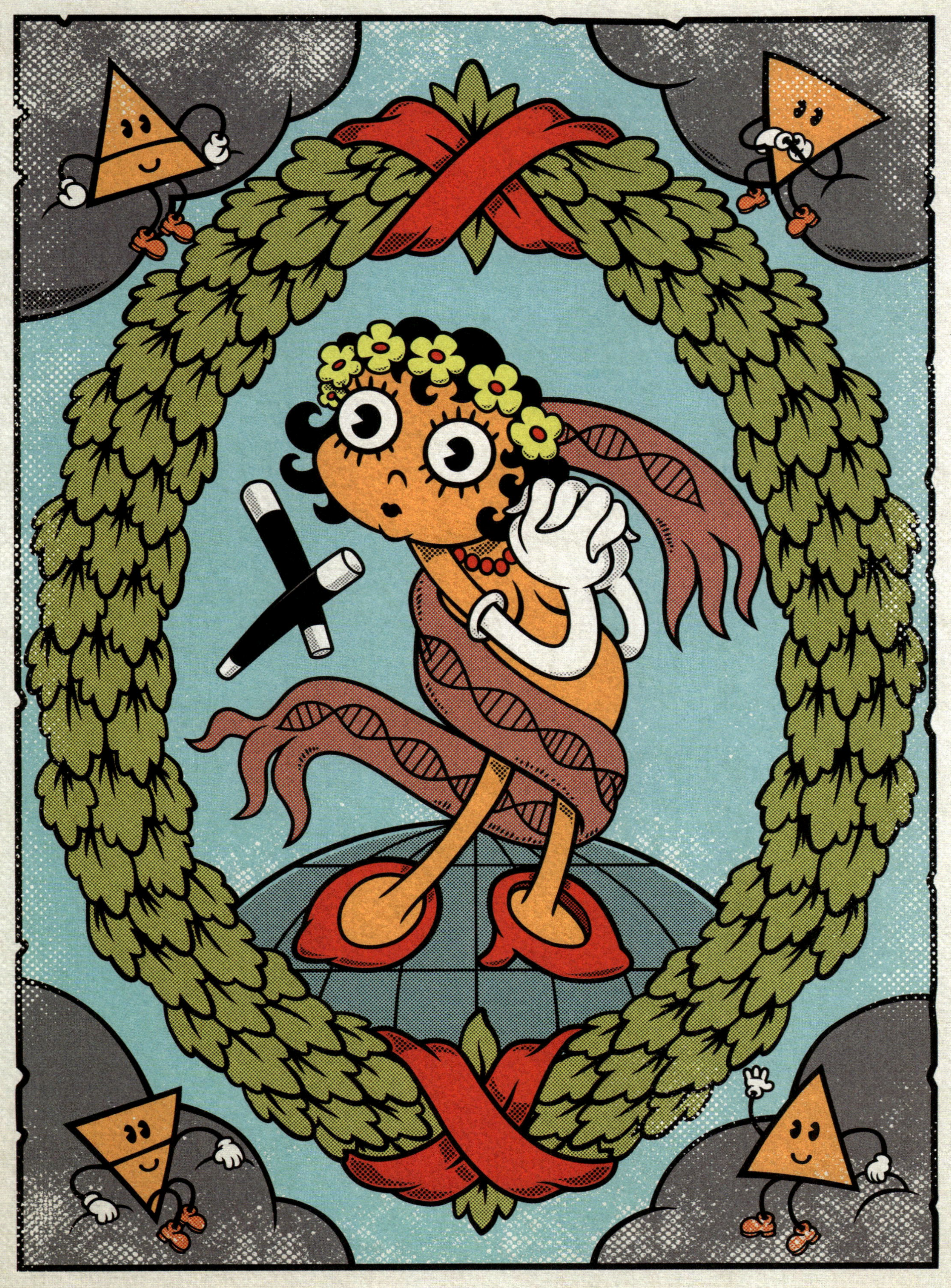

THE WORLD

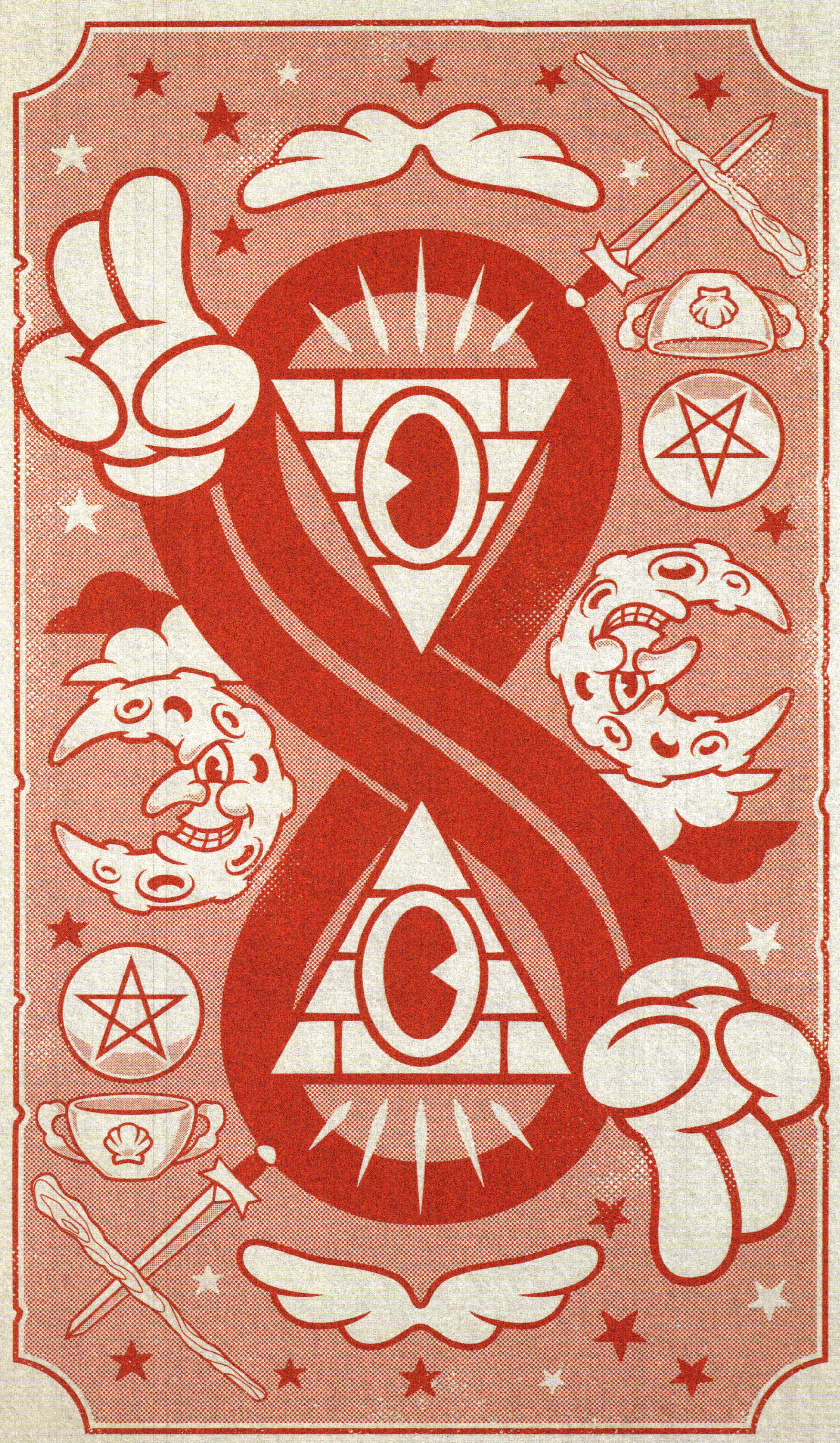

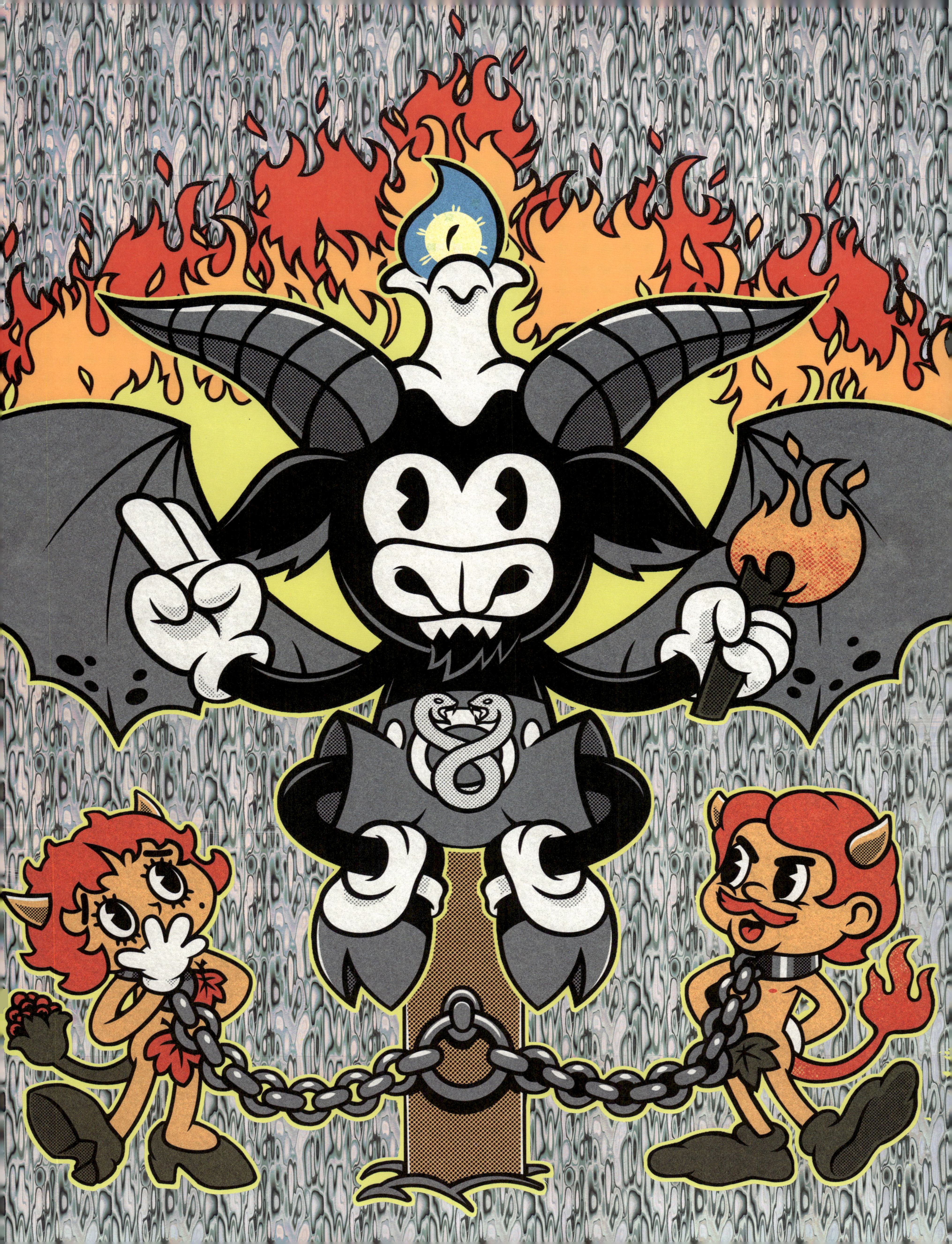

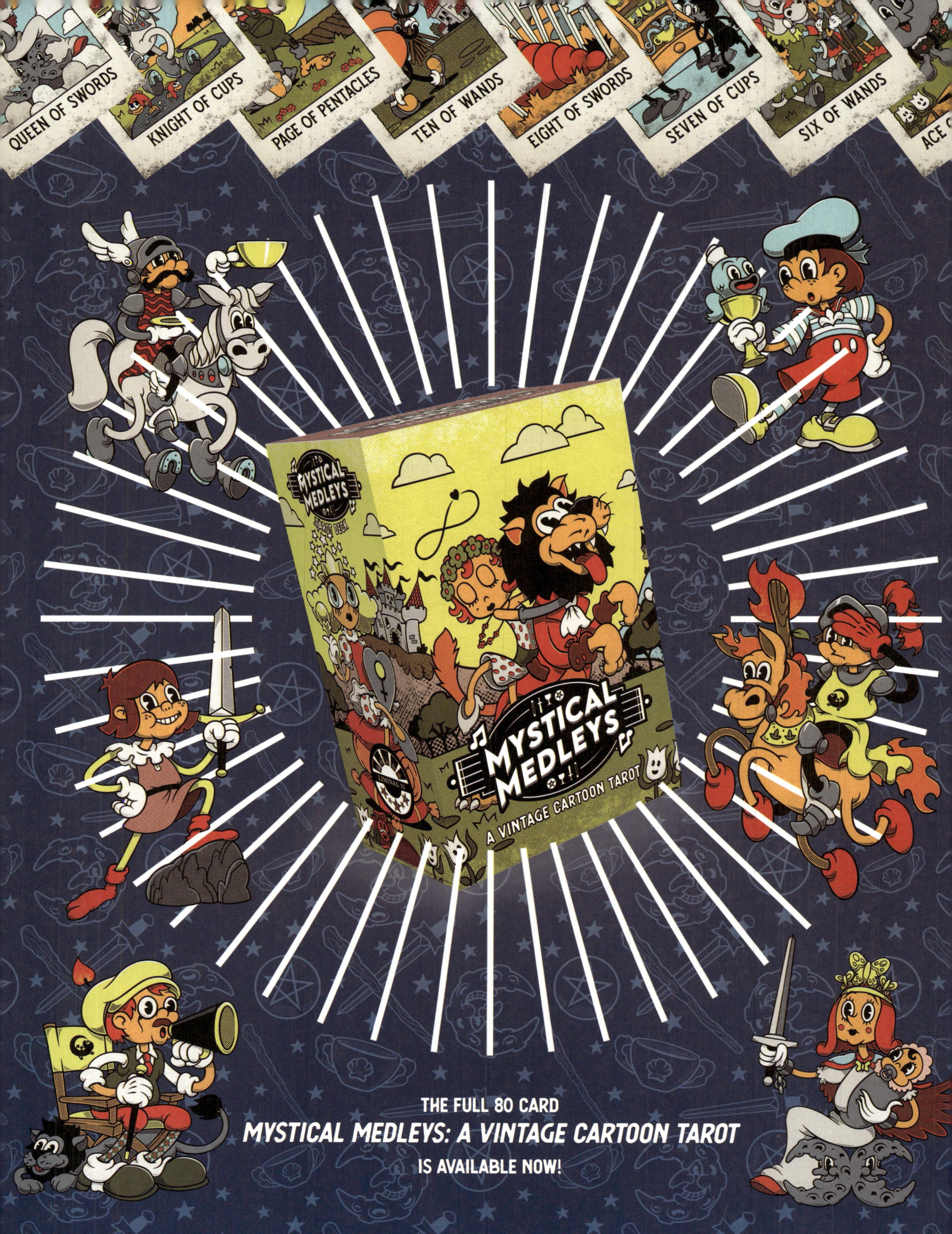
QUEEN OF SWORDS
KNIGHT OF CUPS
PAGE OF PENTACLES
TEN OF WANDS
EIGHT OF SWORDS
SEVEN OF CUPS
SIX OF WANDS
ACE O
MYSTICAL MEDLEYS
MYSTICAL MEDLEYS
A VINTAGE CARTOON TAROT
THE FULL 80 CARD
MYSTICAL MEDLEYS: A VINTAGE CARTOON TAROT
IS AVAILABLE NOW!